Barrel Racing 101

BARREL RACING 101

A Complete Program for Horse and Rider

Marlene McRae

THE LYONS PRESS

Guilford, Connecticut

An imprint of The Globe Pequot Press

To buy books in quantity for corporate use
or incentives, call **(800) 962–0973, ext. 4551,**
or e-mail **premiums@GlobePequot.com.**

The Lyons Press is an imprint of The Globe Pequot Press

10   9   8   7   6   5   4   3   2   1

Printed in the United States of America
Designed by Diane Gleba Hall

ISBN-10: 1-59228-796-4
ISBN-13: 978-1-59228-796-3

Library of Congress Cataloging-in-Publication Data is available on file.

Contents

Part Three
CHAMPION PROGRAM

Part Four
CHAMPION TOOLS

Part Five
CHAMPION EXECUTION

Part Six
PUTTING IT ALL TOGETHER

Introduction

Whatever is worth doing at all is worth doing well.

—LORD CHESTERFIELD

Solving the Performance Horse Puzzle—
How to Find and Use the Secret Pieces

OVER THE YEARS I have often heard the expression that those who win at the highest levels of competition have a secret or two; if other competitors had this knowledge, they too could rise to new heights of success. My goal is that this book will provide the missing secrets to successful barrel racing.

I have developed a philosophy—and a teaching method—based on the idea that a horse and rider's successful development is much like a jigsaw puzzle: the many pieces need to be correctly placed in order for the complete picture to become clear. Identifying each essential puzzle piece leads to success at whatever level each owner/rider wishes to achieve. The basics are the same whether a person wants to trail ride or be the best in the world.

So what is the sport of barrel racing, anyway? A woman and a horse compete against the clock, speeding around three barrels set in a cloverleaf pattern in an arena, usually for less than seventeen seconds. If a barrel is knocked down, a five-second penalty is assigned to the pair. And when the run is over, the electronic clock stops and decides the winner.

There are unlimited barrel racing organizations to join. Each one has their own criteria, and I have listed in the Resource section how to get in contact with them. No matter what level of competitor you are there is a barrel race just for you.

Does it sound simple? Read on! Rodeo spectators don't see the hundreds of practice hours behind every run. They don't see the years of basic horsemanship that define a successful competition pair, or the care and attention to detail behind every successful barrel racing team. But those details define a good barrel run and make a great competition. In the twenty-five years I've spent competing and winning, I've built a list of strategies that I'll share with you, so you can successfully put the barrel racing puzzle together, too.

When you have finished reading this book, I hope that each piece of the puzzle and its important role in successful barrel racing will make the difference in your champion program.

Good luck. I'll see you at the finish line.

—Marlene

Biography

If you have knowledge, let others light their candles in it.

—MARGARET FULLER

I'VE DEVOTED my life to being the best at my profession. I teach, train, compete, and win. My accomplishments and experience allow me to assist others of all ages and ability levels to achieve their goals with their horses.

I grew up in eastern Colorado wanting to be a cowgirl. My parents, Carl and Elma Schiffer, were busy building their ranching, farming, and petroleum businesses, but they always had time to encourage and support my quest to become the best. This lifestyle contributed greatly to my horse and cattle knowledge, as well as my business abilities. Early in my life, I set goals that required the greatest achievement. Being very competitive has driven me to achieve those goals.

At age six I showed registered Shetland ponies against adults in classes like Ladies Fine Harness, Roadster, Western Pleasure, and Halter. I learned early the proper way to prepare and groom a horse for show and performance. Then I joined 4-H and continued my education about horses, judging, and demonstrating.

I was thirteen when I competed at my first Little Britches Rodeo, and I won the All Around Cowgirl award. Now my goals centered on rodeo.

In high school, I was an accomplished saxophonist and traveled around the world playing as member and soloist in selected honor

The Money Roll and me.

bands. I also qualified for the National Little Britches Finals and High School Finals four years in a row, becoming the Colorado High School Rodeo Queen and All Around Rodeo Champion. Music and horses were of equal importance then, though the time was coming for a decision about what I'd focus on.

At Colorado State University, I pursued a more challenging level of rodeo competition, including calf roping. At the regional National Intercollegiate Rodeo Association, I was Breakaway Calf Roping Champion and also the Colorado Amateur Barrel Racing Champion. A business life that included horses looked like the way to go after college.

In 1980, I was drafted for the Denver Stars Rodeo team and won Most Valuable Player. One of my goals was reached when I became the World Champion Barrel Racer in 1983, setting an arena record for fastest time. I continued to rodeo, mainly because of my great horse, Dutch Watch. I knew his abilities could not be put on hold.

In my world championship year, I won more awards than anyone had ever gained at that point. I competed in 120 rodeos that year and was at home for only ten days. During that time I performed for an estimated 13 million live fans and 100 million television viewers. I achieved much more than material rewards and gained knowledge and respect for setting goals and making them happen.

In 1988 came another challenge that I had to dig deep, mentally and physically, to prepare for. The Olympic Games were being held in Calgary, and rodeo was being included for the first time. The United States and Canada rodeo teams were to compete against each other for the coveted gold medals. I won the barrel racing event and the gold medal against the best, including World Champions Charmayne James and Martha Josey. The U.S. team also won the team gold. Winning the two gold medals was the most thrilling accomplishment in my life, though I was very proud when I was inducted into the Cowgirl Hall of Fame in 1995.

I'm pretty proud to have brought fashion to the rodeo world, too. I won the best dressed award at the National Finals Rodeo six times. I've modeled in print ads and posters for Wrangler Jeans, Frontier Airlines, Bailey Hats, Circle Y of Yoakum, Rodeo Video, and Dodge Trucks. I've been on television, including *Good Morning America* and *You Bet Your Life* with Bill Cosby, and radio talk shows, and I've made numerous television commercials for western clothing and skiwear stores.

In twenty-five years, I've taught at over 500 clinics and seminars. Now I produce and star in videotapes on horsemanship and barrel racing, as well as teaching at my own clinics throughout the United States, Brazil, Australia, and Canada. I train and develop horses for sale, endorse selected horse-related products, and develop and market my own mail-order business. In 1990, my business partner and husband, Doug McRae, and I developed World Champion Designs. The core of our retail mail-order business centers on my endorsement of specifically designed and selected products that are strictly developed to protect, enhance, and promote horse soundness, comfort, and performance.

I still compete—and win—at selected rodeo events throughout the United States and Canada. Keeping in the game lets me stay current in the minds of rodeo fans and stay connected with the new bloodlines in the horse world.

As a professional, I've ridden over 100 horses to winnings in professional rodeo competition. My tenth National Finals Rodeo qualification in 2000 capped my career and promoted the stallion that won for me. His name was Fols Classy Snazzy. The past twelve years Doug and I have had a horse partner, friend, and mentor "Margie Denton." Both friends have passed on and I miss them very much. My latest project is to write books with the sole purpose of enhancing the reader's overall knowledge of horses, with an emphasis on complete care essentials for the performance horse.

It gets easier every year to pass up rodeos in order to teach. I love to help others achieve their goals and aspirations. My schedule continues to limit the number of clinics and lessons I teach each year, though. I manage to squeeze in limited enrollment two- and three-day clinics and also offer one-on-one instruction at your facility or at my home on the Lone Tree Ranch in Colorado and Texas.

Throughout my career, I've been lucky to play a part in many different worlds, perhaps because I consider goal-setting and going for it two of my strengths. I never wanted to be one-dimensional.

Marlene at age six showing Crescent Golddust's Trudy.

Life at the top has been good. As a front-runner in women's professional barrel racing, I've been lucky to combine femininity and horsemanship on the road to being a champion rodeo athlete.

Youth, High School and College Career Highlights

- Showing registered Shetland ponies at the age of six.
- State 4-H Champion Horseman and Showman at the age of
  nine. (Held title for four years)
- First rodeo competition at the Little Britches Rodeo in Medi-
  cine Hat, Kansas. (Won the All-Around Cowgirl Award)
- Qualified for National Little Britches Finals and High School
  Finals four consecutive years.
- Colorado High School Rodeo Queen and All Around Rodeo
  Champion.
- Elected National High School Rodeo Secretary.
- Colorado Amateur Barrel Racing Champion.
- Regional National Intercollegiate Rodeo Association Break-
  away Calf Roping Champion.
- WPRA National Finals All Girl qualifier in four events.

Professional Career Highlights

1980–Present
- Drafted by and competed for the Denver Stars Rodeo
  Team (1980)
- Most Valuable Player for World Champion Denver Stars
  Rodeo Team (1980)
- World Champion Barrel Racer (1983)
- Number one draft choice and first woman drafted for PRCA
  Pro Tour Rodeo (1985)
- Member of "The Wrangler/Willie Nelson Outfit" PRCA Pro
  Rodeo Team
- 2X Olympic Gold Medal winner at Calgary Winter Olympics
  (1988)
- 3X Reserve World Champion Barrel Racer (1987,1988,1989)
- 2X National Finals Rodeo Champion Barrel Racer (1983,
  1988)

- 2X Arena record, fastest time at National Finals Rodeo (1983, 1991)
- 10X National Finals Rodeo qualifier (1983–91,2000)
- 5X Calgary Stampede Champion Barrel Racer
- 4X Mountain States Circuit Champion Barrel Racer (1986–89)
- 2X Reserve Champion at Dodge National Circuit Finals Rodeo (1988-89)
- Elected to Board of Directors of the Women's Professional Rodeo Association (1990)
- Inducted into Cowgirl Hall of Fame (1995)
- Instructed at over 500 clinics and seminars (1980–2006)

*Will instruct at over thirty clinics and seminars in 2006 and for years to come.

PART ONE

Champion Rider

*Good luck is a lazy man's estimate
of a worker's success.*

—Unknown

CHAPTER 1

Champion Plan

Winning isn't everything, but wanting to win is.

—VINCE LOMBARDI

Establishing Your Goals and Objectives

*Before you swing a leg over a horse, you should know
why you're swinging it.*

BEFORE YOU can be successful at anything, it is very important to first identify your goals and objectives as you build a champion plan.

First, establish some basics: why you want to barrel race, what you'd like to accomplish, how you plan to get from point A to point B.

Why are you interested in barrel racing? Did you grow up around the sport, following in someone's footsteps? Are you an accomplished horseman looking for something new and fun? Does barrel racing sound like a good choice for a family activity? Do you enjoy trail riding? Are you curious about this fast-paced sport?

How can I get there, if I don't know where I am going?

Next, figure out when and where you are going to use this book's information. This phase of your plan is the "where am I going?" part. Are you going to use it to clean up mistakes in your Pro Rodeo runs when you hit a slump or need to troubleshoot? Are you going to use

Doug, Marlene, and Fols Classy Snazzy winning 5th at the AQHA World Show.

it to learn how to barrel race from the ground up? Are you looking to revamp an existing program, or maybe just tweak one? Are you going to just play around at home with your kids and friends, maybe hitting an occasional playday or gymkhana? Are you getting ready to pull out that two or three-year-old and start him on the pattern? Are you a professional barrel racer trying to build that gold buckle strategy? Whatever your needs, once your goals and objectives are determined, this book will help you understand and use the puzzle pieces.

Next, lay out the steps you will need to make as you move toward your ultimate goal. Sometimes these steps are called "short-term goals." This is the "how to get there" part of your plan and one of the most important steps to keep yourself motivated. If for some reason you don't obtain your ultimate goal, you are still successful each time one of the steps is completed. Motivation is the key to being a champion, so allowing yourself the opportunity to be successful along the way is positive reinforcement that keeps you energized and eager to keep working hard toward that ultimate goal. It is also imperative to set timelines. This encourages you to keep moving toward the end result, chipping away at each step.

If you are a beginner and your ultimate goal is to compete at local jackpots, moving up one division from your starting level, an example of these steps might look something like this:

ACCOMPLISHMENT 1 Enter my first competition at a 4D Jackpot locally by March of this year.
ACCOMPLISHMENT 2 Enter one competition each month from March through November.
ACCOMPLISHMENT 3 Place in the top five of a 4D category at two separate competitions.
ACCOMPLISHMENT 4 By September be running at 3D level.

As you can see, you achieve the first two short-term goals simply by entering. If you should fail on goals three and four, you still have accomplished something and can be proud. That will encourage you to set a new plan in motion when you are done with this one. Staying motivated and positive are requirements to succeed at anything. Making a plan fosters a positive program that will keep you motivated.

Remember that a complete plan has three parts. First is the ultimate goal. Next, determine the specifics of your plan—why, when, where, and how. Third, establish the steps required to achieve that ultimate goal. Now get it down in writing. Keep your plan handy so you can reflect on it often. Your plan might resemble one of these examples:

Example No. 1: **Professional Barrel Racer's Year-long Goal**

I am a competitor with every breath I take.

ULTIMATE GOAL Qualify for my Circuit Finals and finish in the top five.

WHY I want to stay on top and keep winning, ultimately qualifying for my Circuit Finals.
WHEN Every day, to practice, complement, and enhance my current program.

WHERE Pro Rodeos, Divisional Tours, local jackpots, at home, and hopefully at the Circuit Finals!

HOW Give barrel racing my full attention. Make it my top priority. Stay consistent with my program on a daily basis, leave no stone unturned to gain every edge I can on the competition.

Steps to my Goal

STEP 1 Give conditioning and nutrition a bigger role in my program for me and my horse.

STEP 2 Make more competition runs at home and at jackpots before I enter a rodeo.

STEP 3 Qualify for my Circuit Finals.

STEP 4 Place in the top five in my Circuit.

Example No. 2: **Professional Barrel Racer— Having Problems and Wanting Improvement**

I'm really frustrated. I need some help.

ULTIMATE GOAL Understand and correct the problems I am having hitting barrels and getting in the gate. I want to start winning those big checks again and qualify for the Finals. I want my horse to look and feel his best.

WHY I have a nice horse that was once winning, but lately seems to be having lots of problems. He's hitting barrels, won't go in the gate, gets nervous, and won't keep weight on. At home he seems depressed and lethargic. He has also had some soundness issues that may be preventing us from collecting checks.

WHEN I am looking for some immediate help to try and determine where I am going wrong. I want to evaluate my nutritional program and get my horse healthier. I want to understand his soundness issues and the way I have been preparing him.

WHERE At home and at some local jackpots before the next circuit rodeo.

HOW Read Marlene's book and identify the places her experience and knowledge can assist me to clean up these areas of my program. Implement some changes immediately to increase my chances of winning and keeping my horse happy and sound.

Steps to my Goal

STEP 1 Find a good vet, equine dentist, and farrier to be part of my team. I want them to be able to help me stay on top of my horse's health and soundness issues.

STEP 2 Implement a maintenance program to keep my horse comfortable and running his best.

STEP 3 Develop a nutritional program that is detailed and be diligent about keeping my horse healthy. I want to understand his high performance nutritional needs.

STEP 4 Find ways to get my horse moving through the gate without stress. Learn how to keep him relaxed before we run and as we hit the gate.

STEP 5 Cut my current percentage of hitting barrels in half or better.

Example No. 3: Amateur Barrel Racer— Competing at 4D Jackpots

*I look forward to my weekend jackpots,
but I am ready for more.*

ULTIMATE GOAL Start placing consistently and start taking barrel racing more seriously and step it up a notch.

WHY To pick up some new information and work on problems that come up with every barrel horse at different times in their careers. Become a better mental competitor.

WHEN Next year's jackpots.

WHERE In competition situations at various jackpots.

HOW Try to understand some aspects of competition I have never given much thought to by getting some outside help with my horse.

Steps to my Goal

STEP 1 Identify three things I have never given much thought to that may help my barrel racing when I close this book.
STEP 2 Learn how to be tougher mentally when it comes to competing.
STEP 3 Run a $\frac{1}{2}$ second off the winning time by March at my local arena.
STEP 4 Find some new exercises to implement that might help my horse's flexibility.
STEP 5 Place in the second division at the Regional Finals in September.

Example No. 4: Beginner—Starting with the Basics

I don't have a clue about this horse stuff
other than I really want one.

ULTIMATE GOAL I want to buy a horse next year and go to playdays with my friends.

WHY Learn about the proper equipment I need for barrel racing. What and how much to feed my horse. Where do I find a horse? What types of contests are available to get involved in?
WHEN Next fall. My mom promised me a horse after we move.
WHERE Just around my county and in local clubs. I love to trail ride.
HOW Get some basic and general information. I don't have a clue and can't wait to get started—right.

Steps to my Goal

STEP 1 Know what I am looking for when I go to buy a horse and saddle this fall.
STEP 2 Get a broad understanding of what horses are all about, both for pleasure and competing.
STEP 3 Learn the basics of the barrel pattern and how to get my new horse to do it.

STEP 4 Be able to attend a gymkhana with my friend Margie by next summer.

Your complete plan can be as elaborate or simple as you choose, with as many steps as you like. This is your map to success. The examples give you an idea of how you can approach your goals and objectives, so be creative. Add in some inspirational sayings that may help to motivate you, and keep it somewhere you can refer to. Again, positive accomplishments, even small ones, keep you moving forward and eager to pursue and accomplish big things.

PART TWO

Champion Horse

*I say to parents, especially wealthy parents; Don't give your son money.
As far as you can afford it, give him horses. No one ever came to grief—
except honorable grief—through riding horses. No hour of life
is lost that is spent in the saddle.*

—SIR WINSTON CHURCHILL (1874–1965)

CHAPTER 2

Finding a Champion

Nothing great was ever achieved without enthusiasm.

—RALPH WALDO EMERSON

Now THAT you have established your goals and objectives on paper, finding your champion horse should be much easier. You clearly know where you want to go in barrel racing and what your own expectations are. Now we move on to the four-legged participant in the game.

Over the years, I have received lots of questions about the process of buying or replacing horses. Here is an example to get us started with the slew of questions, concerns, and hurdles.

QUESTION I recently lost my horse and want to replace him. This is a very hard decision, and since I have started to look for another horse, I have been surprised at the volume of specialized horses on the market and the prices. I know you get what you pay for, but I am not looking for a "Pro" caliber horse, just a solid one. I am very confused and just don't know how to go about locating a horse to suit me and my needs. I put a wanted ad on the Internet and was flooded with calls. Any tips you could give me would help. I don't think that you can go ride a horse one or two times and know if the horse is right for you. How do you handle this situation in trying a horse and what do you look for when doing it?

ANSWER When searching for a horse, you should have a complete game plan. Write a list of what you want, such as your price range, preferred age, what events you wish to compete in, do you prefer a mare or a gelding, etc. Your wish list will dictate where you can start the search.

When you have a game plan written out, contact a person who has experience and credentials. This type of person can assist you in your endeavor. Ask questions based on your wish list prior to riding the horse and compare this with what the owner had told you previously. If the information you were told is incorrect, chances are any other information supplied is also incorrect. It is a buyer-beware market. Credentials of horse and owner will help you with your decisions.

Do not expect a seller to allow multiple rides on a horse you are trying. Also, do not expect a seller to permit you to take the horse to multiple competitions. This is risky at best for the horse and the owner. Personally, I like the customer to come to the ranch and ride the horse they are interested in while we videotape the test ride. Then we can view the video and discuss the customer's impressions. If riding the horse in a competition is requested, then I will arrange for the horse to be delivered to a local competition where the customer can compete on the horse. I believe this is sufficient in determining whether the horse is capable or not.

The essential criteria are that the horse has good conformation and this horse must be sound (determined by a qualified veterinarian); it must be broke correctly and be able to demonstrate its abilities without resistance. I see so many people purchase horses based on emotions rather than fact, which only leads to disappointment and grief. Take your time, evaluate your options, and do not buy based on emotion.

• • •

IF YOU don't already have a horse or have never purchased one for barrel racing, this section of the book will assist you in making sound choices when looking for that champion horse. You will need to know how to go about finding horses to look at, what factors to note during

This is Dutch Watch, the horse I won the WPRA World Championship, two Olympic Gold medals, and eight trips to the National Finals Rodeo on.

the selection process, and how to get a professional to assess your buy in a prepurchase exam.

So let's get started with our prepurchase plan. Begin with setting a budget. The best way is to look at the market. Because you now know what level of competition you expect to compete at, doing some research will help you understand what that level of horse is currently bringing.

If you are looking for a 1D horse, read some classifieds or look at some online sources. You will quickly be able to determine a base range for current prices being sought and spent on the 1D horse. The same applies for the 4D horse or a trail riding horse. Regardless of the caliber or discipline, you need to establish what the market is bearing. If at this time you can't afford the level horse you hoped for, you need to either reevaluate your goals and objectives or find a way to increase the amount of money you can spend. Remember it costs the same to feed a cheap horse as it does to feed a expensive horse!

Don't fall into a trap where you spend more than you should have and then can't afford proper care and upkeep on that horse. Don't be an emotional buyer. Establish a budget and stick to it. You want to give this horse every chance possible to be the best he can be. If you have to skimp on his feed or care, you're not doing that. Be smart about it. Have a plan, have a budget and stay with it.

When you're tempted to go look at that horse out of your range, remind yourself that the purchase is only the beginning of your responsibility to him.

When you're setting a budget, realize that you may be able to talk a seller down, but don't count on it. Often the horses that you can wheel and deal on aren't worth the money asked. That is why the owner will come down. The horse that we're looking for will generally be coming from a seller that knows his value. Not always, but frequently, the owner who is unwilling to come down in price knows the horse is a good one. Of course, there are those shrewd sellers who know how to play the game, but it is something to keep in mind.

If you do want to try and wheel and deal on a more expensive horse, know what you can spend and be up front with the seller. Don't put four runs on a horse you know you can't afford hoping you'll be able to *maybe* talk his price down. Be courteous to the seller during this process and let the seller know where you're coming from.

So you know what you want and how much you have to spend. Where do you start? There are two basic ways to buy. Search yourself and then evaluate privately owned horses. Or you might hire someone like myself with credentials to look for a horse for you. There is an up- and downside to each.

If you go it alone, you will be relying on your own skill and intuition. Additionally you will have to negotiate with sellers yourself. The upside is that you may save some money in the end, if you make a wise choice.

If you go to a credentialed professional agent to find a horse, realize they will make a commission, usually 10–20 percent. You are paying for a service, and with that service you will hopefully have the peace of mind that your purchase is a good one. You should also increase your chances for finding a successful match. A professional agent has seen it all and understands what is necessary for a purchase to work out for both the buyer and seller. They normally have access to more horses, too. I see hundreds of horses each month. Because it is my job, naturally I have access to many prospects and solid horses and contacts known to be trustworthy.

When buying through an agent, expect he or she to help you learn to ride this horse, give you the bit the horse has been riding in, and help you sell the horse if the horse you choose does not work out a year or two from now. If the agent is not willing to do these three simple things, then find another person you want to do business with.

Now you know what you want, how much it should cost, what you can spend, and how you will search the market. Let's move on to the particulars of your requirements and needs.

Whether you are going it alone or going to a professional agent, make a checklist. Start with your goals and budget. Now establish the other particulars like age, sex, and size. The better you plan and do your homework, the less likely you will make a purchase mistake.

Example No. 1

What is my goal for this horse? 4-H and gymkhana.

How long do I need this horse to last? Until my daughter graduates and goes to college—four years.

What age range am I looking for? I'd like a horse between ten and fourteen. When my daughter graduates, it would be okay to retire this horse.

What sex do I need? I have three geldings already and don't like messing around with mares. A gelding is surely preferred.

What events or uses? Barrels, poles, trail, equitation, and pleasure riding.

How much can I spend? In order to have plenty of money to give this horse an advantage in care, I have about $4,500.

Here is your checklist: *Ten to fourteen years old, gelding, $4,500 range, for local competition.*

Example No. 2

What is my goal for this horse? Open horse for jackpots and pro-rodeo.

How long do I need this horse to last? As long as possible.

What age range am I looking at? eight to twelve.

What sex do I need? I'd prefer a mare, but she must be easy to be around. That way if she got hurt, there is always a way to recover my money by either selling her as a broodmare or breeding her myself.

What events or uses? Specifically barrels, but if I ever resell I would like the benefit of her also running poles or roping. Around the ranch it's also nice to know she'd be able to work cattle.

How much can I spend? In order to have plenty of money to give this horse an advantage in care, I have about $25,000.

Here is your checklist: *Eight to twelve years old, mare, $25,000 range for open, pro-rodeo caliber horse.*

•   •   •

ONCE YOU have a checklist and have determined which route you will take in buying, let's walk the "go-it-alone" path. Start with talking to people who have had good luck with their purchases. If you see a horse that has what you're looking for at a barrel race, go up and talk to the owner. Find out where the horse came from, who trained him, and other particulars.

If you go to private parties to buy, take someone with you. Sometimes we overlook things. Having that second set of eyes is helpful. Be patient and thorough when you are looking. Don't fall into the "someone is coming tomorrow to look at him" trap. If this horse is meant to be, he will still be there when you're ready. Avoid an impulse buy. It's a buyer-beware market, and your diligence will help you come out well.

The Game Plan

Set up a time to go look at the horse. This can be at the owner's home arena; you want to see this horse at his best. Before you ride this horse, confirm the price, look at the registration papers for exact age, and then carefully look at this horse's conformation. If you have serious reservations at this time, say thank you and leave. If all the above is satisfactory, continue assessing the overall conformation carefully. You'll find all the information you need to judge conformation in the next chapter, so read it carefully to prepare. If you are okay with what you see, then ask the owner to ride the horse first and demonstrate the usual warm-up. Notice how well broke the horse is. Watch how the horse stops; is it easy or does the owner have to pull hard on the reins? Does the horse move off leg pressure? Is the owner wearing spurs? If not, ask if you can. Pay attention to the horse's ability to flex and bend; is it the same both directions? Watch the owner work the horse on barrels and note if the horse stays relaxed. If the horse is nervous and does not like to work slowly, it will take longer to get to know the horse, especially if you are a beginner barrel racer. It is much easier to get with a horse if they will allow you to progress at your own speed.

Now it is time for you to get on and get a feel for the horse. Remember to take deep breaths and relax as much as possible for your sake and the horse's. Ride around the arena and test your controls. Stop and back up a few times; at the trot, make some pretend barrel turns to see how much you have to pull on the reins to turn a small circle. Then lope the horse in a large circle, flexing the head to the center of the circle. Pay attention to any resistance to any maneuver you ask of him. Then take him around the barrel pattern at a trot, paying attention to the pocket size; does he slow down before the turn like he should, or does he speed up in the turn? Then lope him through the barrels, stopping at each one to see if you have some brakes or whether this makes the horse mad. I am sure the owner will be calling out instructions. Try to listen to them, but really listen to the horse you are on.

When discussing this horse with the owner, do not stand down at the end of the barrel pattern. Step off the horse or ride over to the side of the arena away from the starting point of the barrel pattern, which is the hot zone for a horse, where they take off like a rocket. They cannot read our minds, so most competition horses are ready to give 100 percent every time and will become frustrated by standing around. It is really hard to show a finished barrel horse to prospective buyers, because the horse does not know what is going on. The normal routine has been changed, and this can make some horses upset.

Next, make a run on this horse. Feel the horse under you and pay attention to how he did his job. If you like what you felt, then arrange for a second session at another arena. It does not need to be at an event. Just going to an unfamiliar arena will create enough change that you should feel any problems away from home this horse may have. You can do this all in one day if time is an issue, making sure you're videotaping all this so you can review it later. Go and sleep on it and if you want to pursue the sale or not let the owner know in a timely manner.

The next step is the prepurchase examination if you choose to do one. Ask your veterinarian to refer you to an equine clinic in the area. Set up the appointment and ask the owner/agent to meet you there with the horse. I cover this in a later chapter. This is the closing of the deal, have your money in order and take possession at this time. Congratulations, you have a new horse and friend, and the fun has just begun.

Often you will find there are horsemen out there that do pride themselves on their reputation for finding and selling good horses. At the same time, know there are twice as many that don't. I pride myself on finding horses that fit the rider and resell horses someone bought from me previously. I can do this because I know there is nothing wrong with the horse. If there was, I would have never sold him the first time. That is the reputation I am talking about. Someone who is a professional horse person understands reputation is everything.

I feel contracts are important, to ensure everyone is on the same page. The contract should include price, form of payment, and any special agreements you may want. The seller and agent have one, and the agent and buyer have one. You can write these between yourselves, sign, date, and each one keeps a copy. Permanent Registration Papers and signed transfer of ownership are exchanged after all funds are deposited in the seller's account. Some states require a brand inspection done before the horse is transported to the new owner. The contract and brand inspection are your bill of sale, and will be helpful if you choose to insure your horse.

CHAPTER 3

Champion Traits

Best is a relative term. There is no best animal for every situation.
The kind of animal that works best in one environment may be quite
different from the optimal in another set of circumstances.

—RICHARD M. BOURDON

Pedigree and Breeding

NOW WE are ready to get started looking for our champion. We have our plan, our checklist, and somebody to help us search, either our credentialed professional or someone to help us look potential purchases over. There are several things that must be evaluated in shopping for that special athlete. Let's talk about them.

A good horse can do anything. A great one proves to be exceptional in many areas. My great horse, Dutch Watch, was a winner in everything he did. He was AAA on the track as a two-year-old and was tenth at the Snaffle Bit Futurity in Reno. I won the WPRA World Championship on him in 1983 in barrel racing and went on to eight National Finals Rodeo qualifications with him. My husband Doug roped calves on him for nearly a year, winning over $10,000 on him at nineteen years old. He proved himself in the racing, cutting, and reining worlds, and the calf roping and the barrel racing world. He was everything you want in one package—that is what we are looking for, ultimately, that champion that can do anything that we need them to. To find a champion-caliber horse, there can't be much compromise. An outstanding individual needs to be great in many different areas.

Let's start with breeding and pedigree. Look at the pedigree, not because this horse can read and see he is supposed to be a champion, but because there are years of genetics there. Some bloodlines may be proven and some may not. If those genes are strong and deep, with proven performers, your chances of success have already increased.

Talk to the owner or the breeder listed on the papers about each individual dam and sire. Most owners and breeders are proud of their bloodlines and can offer you lots of information. This is an important piece of the puzzle in that it can tell us what to expect from a horse.

Most importantly, look at the dam. Too much emphasis is put on the stallion alone. You need to realize that the mare contributes 60 percent of the foal's genetic material. She is bringing two X chromosomes to the offspring, while that stallion is bringing either an X or Y to determine its sex. I am not saying that stallion pedigree is not very important, because it is. What I am saying is do not overlook the dam. She will also contribute a great deal in behavioral traits. That foal learned how to respond to stimulus from the mother. If she was extremely spooky, this foal has been taught from day one to be leery of everything. If that mare

Marlene and Chicks Beduino, a leading race and barrel horse sire.

is quiet and loves to be petted, that foal's attitude is going to reflect that. So find out some background about this horse's sire and especially its dam.

Ask to see pictures of the dam and sire if available. The stallion is going to have a strong influence on the structural makeup of his offspring. Look at him in person if you can or study a picture. Pay attention to his substance of bone and ask a lot of questions about that stallion's history as both a producer and performer.

A prospect's breeding should contain a performance background of some sort. Look in that pedigree for genetic characteristics that will benefit this horse. A barrel horse needs to be able to run, yes, but he also needs to be able to stop and turn. You will find your best genetic crosses will have a cow horse influence. A pedigree with both cow horse influence and some Thoroughbred can provide the ability to run and contribute stamina, making a tougher individual.

We are seeing a lot of running Quarter Horse genes in the barrel horse industry, with an emphasis on speed indexes. A speed index is important when it comes to sire influences. Speed index ratings compare a horse's race time to the three fastest winning times for the same distance run each year for the past three years at a particular track. The average of the nine race times (to the nearest 1/1000 (.001) of a second) will represent a speed index rating of 100. If a horse matches that average speed, he achieves a speed index of 100 for that race. Perhaps this plays no role in how fast an individual you may be trying can run barrels, but it is an indicator that a horse is genetically predisposed for speed.

You may also hear that he or she has "a Racing Register of Merit" when discussing pedigree. This award is achieved by obtaining a speed index of 80 or higher. One more term you might hear while talking genetics and breeding is "Superior Race Horse." A horse that is awarded a Superior Race Horse is an AQHA horse which has earned 200 racing points. A horse awarded a Supreme Race Horse will be an AQHA horse that has achieved each of the following: earnings of $500,000 or more; winner of two open grade stakes races (G1), or two races of grade 1 historical significance prior to 1983; and winner of ten races. These are the most frequently used terms you may hear about a horse's family pedigree if a racing influence is present in the pedigree.

Many genetic lines have become specialized over the last ten to fifteen years. If you're looking for a performance horse, don't buy halter genetics. Halter genetics were developed to stand, trot, and look pretty, but not for agility and speed. Of course, this does not mean a horse with some of these genes can't win in barrel racing. It means statistically, their chances are less, especially if the pedigree is riddled with them.

Because we can't ride young horses or prospects, we can only make an educated guess as to what they will be. Pedigree can lend us some help in determining that.

If you aren't looking for a young prospect, pedigree is not as important. Consider it, and then go on to the individual itself for evaluation.

Once you are looking at a horse approximately three years old and above, judge him for what he is, not what his papers say.

Frequently you will hear, "He's a half brother to so-and-so's world champion." Don't give this much weight. Just because my brother is a professional ball player doesn't mean I should be one too. Assess each individual against himself. This is probably one of the most misunderstood concepts in genetics. If all you had to do was breed a world champion to another world champion to get another world champion, there would be champions on every block. Consider pedigree in older horses, but make your final decision by evaluating the individual.

Conformation

This chapter's vital importance rests on the principle that proper *conformation* is the basic building block of any accomplished champion. First, it is important to realize that every horse has strong and weak points of conformation. No horse is perfect; many horses, even champions, can excel with flaws. However, conformation cannot be altered.

Each horse has physical flaws and assets that play a direct role in performance. In any equine discipline, there are physical characteristics that assist and/or hinder optimum performance. To maximize the success of both horse and rider, it is imperative that you understand conformation and how its form applies to the functions demanded in barrel racing. The closer your individual is to the ideal form required for a specific type of locomotion, the easier execution of that locomotion will be. Proper structure allows the performance horse to maximize potential with ease and enthusiasm. When something is easy, it's also enjoyable. With enjoyment comes a willingness to perform. If your horse has unlimited athletic potential because his physical body allows him to run barrels with ease, the sky is the limit.

The horse is made of several interdependent systems. The skeletal system is the basic framework. The joints serve as connectors, shock absorbers, and linkage. Tendons and ligaments function as cords and connectors, while muscles are the source of power. The simple yet complex machine of the living horse has one basic goal: to move this mass of living material from one point to another.

Like any machine, all components must be in balance to function with efficiency. The mass of a machine, in this case the horse, must be in balance with its supporting structure. The idea of balance depends on a center of gravity. The shape and motion of what the machine or horse is doing will dictate where the center of gravity lies. In our equine athlete, the center of gravity is generally located near the center of the rib cage. The forelimbs are therefore forced to bear 65 percent of the horse's total weight. Thus the head and neck of the horse is used to balance this mass as it moves, adjusting for the center of gravity. Likewise, balance, in general structure, is always a true center of gravity. When imbalanced, locomotion is greatly affected.

Although some horses perform well even with physical imperfections, a lack of structural balance will directly affect physical ability and influence the likelihood of injury, in turn, playing a large role in any equine athlete's longevity. Structural design flaws generally lead to unnecessary and uneven wear, eventually resulting in injury and retirement. Pain accompanies wear and injury and is reflected in a horse's disposition, mental attitude, and the desire to perform. No matter how hard the individual with flawed conformation tries, his

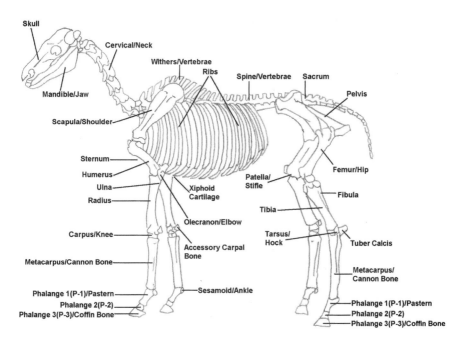

The horse's skeletal system.

body is not mechanically capable of executing maneuvers at the same level of effectiveness, comfort, and soundness that the horse with better physical structure can. Without the proper race car, even the most qualified and experienced driver will not win the Indy 500. Similarly, without the appropriate equine athlete, even the most qualified and experienced barrel racer will not achieve long-term success.

Although specifics vary, selection based on conformation is a necessity in any type of equine performance. The physical composition required of a reining horse as he slides down the arena are the same traits that prevent him from running as fast as a racehorse can or jumping as high as a steeplechase horse. The reverse can be said of the racehorse and jumping horse. Their conformation, although exceptional for what they do, would prevent them from sliding down the pen like the reining horse.

All of these ideas are the foundation for the scientific principle known as "form to function." The horse's form must support the rider's demands for mechanical locomotion. In the demanding, fast-paced sport of barrel racing, specific physical attributes are vital for proper execution of the pattern, which includes short, hard sprints, quickly gathered momentum, precise body flexion, lateral movements of the front and hindquarters in order to reverse direction, and rapid acceleration. To add difficulty to this high energy event, we often ask our equine partners to perform in less than perfect conditions, such as a long trailer haul, poor ground conditions, hot or cold weather, and a screaming crowd that interferes with the acoustics he uses to adjust his own body.

This is why certain physical properties absolutely cannot be compromised in selecting the champion barrel horse. While some of these areas are less important in their role for successful performance, each is a piece of the puzzle. My evaluation of a horse's physical ability to perform in barrel racing begins with several categories. In each category, there are several additional items to evaluate. In an attempt to teach which conformational flaws and assets should be valued most and which ones you can be more lenient with, I have rated them each on a scale from 1 to 10. A rating of "1" means this aspect of conformation has a minimal impact on successful performance, while a rating of "10" will indicate substantial importance crucial to success and longevity.

As we evaluate the barrel horse's "form to function" requirements, my system is documented with detailed examples, pictures, and descriptions. My step-by-step explanation coupled with illustrations of these ideas will make perfect sense to the beginning barrel racer.

Let's start with those categories I feel are the most deserving of a "10" rating in the selection and evaluation of your barrel racing athlete. Even slight deviations from proper structure in these areas will eventually result in unsoundness and/or lack of performance. Whether it costs you on the clock or at the vet clinic, the areas I rate a "10" are of the utmost importance in an athlete's ability to use his form for the function we call barrel racing.

Let's begin at the ground level and work our way up; after all, even a house requires a strong, sturdy foundation to last any length of time.

10—The Hooves: The foundation of the champion barrel horse

The equine hoof has nearly thirty-four working parts and is clearly the most complex working mechanism in the entire skeletal structure of the horse.

The average barrel horse weighs between 1,000 and 1,200 pounds, and each hoof supports an enormous amount of weight. In addition, the hoof is required to absorb the concussion from each step that strikes the ground. Add in the weight of the rider, the inertia and force driven down each limb during high performance maneuvers, and the frequent reality of less than perfect ground conditions, and a key piece of your puzzle is in constant jeopardy.

Hooves need to be large, round, and sturdy. If a house has a foundation smaller than the large, heavy structure upon it, eventually it

would start falling apart. The bigger the circumference of the hoof, the more surface area there is to absorb concussion and allow energy to leave the limbs. With this said, give priority to big, round, sturdy feet, as they are the foundation of the champion barrel horse.

A large, round, well-balanced hoof.

10—The Forelegs: The shock absorbers
in the champion barrel horse

Barrel horse legs need to have substance and be straight and centered. The bones need to be large and have a flat, wide look when you view this horse from the side. Although the leg bone is cylinder-shaped, when the tendons and ligaments have the proper substance to go with that bone, a flat appearance results. If you see a round, little leg, the support is not going to be there. As you know, we cannot get replacement parts. The bone above the knee, the radius bone, needs to connect to the center of the knee. The cannon bone, the bone below the knee, should drop from the center of the knee, tying into the center

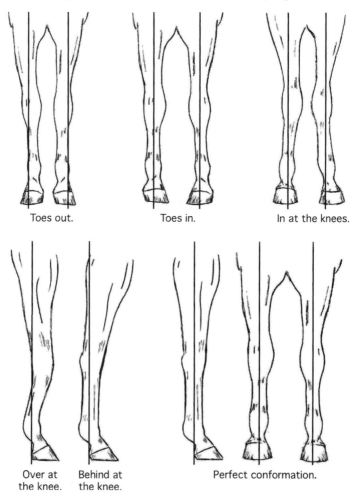

Toes out.   Toes in.   In at the knees.

Over at   Behind at   Perfect conformation.
the knee.   the knee.

of the ankle and through the center of the hoof. This ensures efficient function of the joints all the way down the leg and out through the hoof, allowing the energy and concussion of movement a straight passage. The energy that muscles and joints generate during locomotion needs to exit down that limb and out through the heel of the foot. If any of the bones are off center, the pressure will be off to one side of the knee or ankle or hoof, wearing the joints unevenly.

The harsh facts are that we are already involved in an event that is asking a horse to run straight and then rapidly slow down and turn. When a horse is turning, he is turning on the sides of his joints. He is not using them like God intended them to be used. We have to start out with a very correct and balanced horse, so that when we do ask him to use his joints at an angle, we can maximize his longevity. Because it takes a long time to train a horse, we are looking for horses that will last us for eight or nine years in the competitive world. Start with a well-conformed horse that has the potential to stay sound, and you will end up with more years of use.

So now that you have assessed the horse's basic leg structure and how it relates to his joints under stress, let's move up the leg from the hoof.

A pastern with moderate length is favored because of its ability to diffuse impact. However, an excessively long pastern puts extreme tension on the tendons and ligaments of the back of the leg, predisposing a horse to bowed tendons and suspensory ligament injuries. In the horse with excessively long pasterns, the suspensory is strained because the fetlock is unable to straighten as the horse loads the limb with his weight. He is predisposed to injuries in speed events where the sesamoids are under extreme pressure from the pull of the suspensory. The excessive drop of the fetlock puts more stress on the pastern and coffin joints, which in turn sets up the perfect conditions for arthritis. An excessively long pastern also delays acceleration, which is undesirable in barrel horses.

The horse with a short, steep pastern brings different complications to the table. A short, steep pastern is less shock absorbing and also contributes to a short stride. The sharp turns demanded in barrel racing and the concussion this area of the leg receives open the door for sidebone, ringbone, and navicular disease. Use these three basic rules to assess your prospect's pasterns. First, the pastern angle should match that of the shoulder. Second, a long pastern is considered to be more than three-

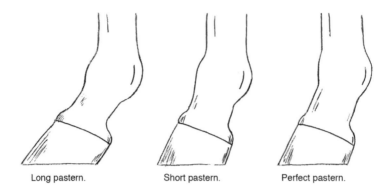

Long pastern.   Short pastern.   Perfect pastern.

quarters the length of the cannon bone. Third, a short pastern is less than one-half the length of the cannon bone. These three concepts should help you judge any possible flaws in the length of the pastern. Again, moderation of the length of the pastern and a balanced angular slope are best. Personally, I would choose a long pastern over a short one.

As we continue up the front legs, next is the cannon bone. Look for a short, sturdy cannon bone. A short cannon bone is desired in any performance horse. It enables an efficient pull of the tendons across the back of the knee or point of hock to move the limb forward and back, while reducing the weight of the lower leg. Reduced weight requires less muscular effort to move the limbs. This in turn will contribute to speed, stamina, soundness, and ability. The short cannon bone improves the ease and power of the force generated by the muscles of a long forearm, our next bone.

The forearm, or radius, should be long. A short cannon bone and long forearm combine for maximum leverage, producing length of stride and speed. If this bone is short, speed is compromised. The horse with a short forearm will have to exert more muscular effort. He will also exhibit knee action, wasting energy in upward motion instead of forward motion.

Next is the humerus or arm bone. From the elbow to the point of the shoulder, the humerus should be 50 to 60 percent of the length of the scapula, or shoulder bone. This is because it acts as a lever. It is medium in length and helps dictate the length of stride. If the humerus is long, the elbow will be beneath the middle of the withers. The front legs will appear to be set behind the shoulder instead of in front of the shoulder. Humerus length dictates how tightly the elbow and lower joints can bend and reach for extension, which affects lateral movement, efficiency, length of stride, and speed. This bone provides a scaffold for long muscle attachments to contract with greater force, increasing power and speed. Again we are looking for depth of bone and muscle and how it ties into the structure above and below it. It all should flow together with balance, from the ground, up the leg, into the shoulder, and throughout the entire horse.

The front legs are rated as a "10" because they are the shock absorbers in the champion barrel horse. The hindquarters and hind legs are evaluated a little later in this chapter.

9—The Neck: The balance pendulum of the champion barrel horse

The ideal neck must be sleek and long to balance the body of the horse. As mentioned in the beginning of this chapter, the neck is used mostly to balance this moving mass of a horse and maintain the center of gravity. The neck's length therefore dictates the way a horse uses his front legs and shoulders, particularly for stride or reach. If a horse's neck is too short, the animal will be able to stop his forward momentum quickly, but he will not have a long stride.

The ability to extend stride will always be ruled first by the horse's conformation. A short stride is obviously not conducive to speed and makes it difficult for a horse to pull himself around a barrel. Additionally, horses with thick necks do not have flexibility, which is critical for lateral movement, balance, and body flexion in barrel racing horses.

In general, the horse must be built in proportion. A short, inflexible neck will generally tie into a short shoulder, short body, and short hip. Be aware of the other extreme: a neck that is too thin, known as ewe-necked. This conformation allows a horse to arch his neck backward, resulting in a very high-headed horse. This impairs a horse's ability to watch where he is going or use his front end effectively. A horse needs balance to execute various athletic maneuvers. Forward weight is

A perfect neck.

necessary to balance the rest of the large body in motion. Keep it in proportion and use these tools to evaluate proper length.

It is also imperative to have a neat, clean throatlatch. Everything passes through this area that the horse needs: food, air, blood, nerves, and glands. If the horse has a thick or coarse throatlatch, when he tries to give to the bit and tuck his nose even slightly, his vital supplies are compromised. And we all can imagine what trying to run while being choked might feel like. I'm getting dizzy just thinking about that.

It is also important to note that restricted air intake decreases oxygenation of the blood, which leads to muscle fatigue and longer recovery times, emphasizing the importance of a horse's ability to breathe properly. If you can place three to four fingers between the jaw bones of your horse, under most circumstances he has adequate width through his throatlatch.

Finally, good conformation means that the neck ties into his chest and shoulder smoothly and neatly, creating a balanced, clean look. A neat tie into the shoulder and chest will insure balance and freedom of the shoulders, another important aspect of the lateral moves used in barrel racing. Neck conformation is important. It facilitates length of stride, balances the center of gravity, and dictates the flexibility of movement. The neck is rated a "9" because it is the balance pendulum of the champion barrel horse.

9—Size: The first factor of execution in the champion barrel horse

A horse that is overly tall will have a harder time sprinting for short distances. He will require a longer distance to reach maximum locomotion. A large horse is heavier, creating more concussion on his feet, joints, and muscles, resulting in more physical unsoundness, soreness, and exertion. These will contribute to problems in training and enjoyment in his job. When choosing a horse, the size of the rider must be considered. A 100-pound person can ask a 14.2-hand horse to carry her across the finish line with success. However, a 175-pound person should rethink the purchase of a horse that size. A 125-pound person with a 38" inseam would be unrealistic choosing a shorter horse. Her spurs are useless dangling below the rib cage. A long-legged rider needs a horse with a deep heart girth, so that when you apply leg pressure, you make contact with the horse's sides.

Don't ask a small horse to run with an anvil on his back when instead you could be likened to a brick aboard a bigger horse. Pick a horse that fits the rider. The rider's height, weight, and length of arms and legs all play a role in a successful ride.

Since we are speaking about the rider's ability to execute certain tasks, let's talk about an example of it. Think of the length of the rider's arms in comparison to the length of a horse's neck for a moment. You can imagine that a rider with short arms or a short torso would have trouble getting to the proper place on her reins while riding a really big, long-necked horse. She won't be able to be as effective as a rider with longer arms and torso, on this horse. Why? Because she can never reach close enough to the horse's mouth to get the proper bend. So, choose a horse that complements your physical traits. Just as the horse's neck and shoulder should be in proportion to each other, you should be in proportion to your horse. Pick a horse to complement you, not hinder your ability to be effective on his back. Likewise don't hinder his ability because you are too large, tall, or awkward up there. Continue the rule of balance. You are an extension of his own physical body while aboard.

8—The Shoulders: Crucial to smooth, efficient range of motion in the champion barrel horse

The shoulders must be wide, long, and sloping. There must be width between the front legs. This width allows good lateral movement and control during a barrel turn. Every world champion barrel horse that I have ever seen has had substantial width between the shoulders. The shoulder bone, or scapula, should be long and angular, with adequate slope between the scapula and the arm bone, or humerus. It should appear closer to parallel than vertical. A steep, short scapula will produce a shorter stride that is jarring to both the rider and the horse's own joints and body. Because the forearm,

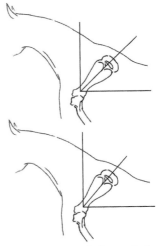

Top: A nice, angled scapula bone known as the shoulder. Bottom: A very straight shoulder.

or radius, allows the leg to extend forward beneath the shoulder, the length of each is both corresponding and reliant of the other. Although many people think stride is determined by the length of the legs, the shoulder is the basis of the stride. You want a long shoulder, or scapula bone, to connect to the humerus, to produce smooth, efficient range of both forward and lateral motion in the champion barrel horse.

7—Eyes: For awareness of the surroundings of the champion barrel horse

The eye of the horse is one of the largest in the entire animal kingdom. It is twice the size of the human eye and bigger than either the elephant or the whale. It is a light-intensifying device with a layer that reflects light back onto the retina, making the horse much better at seeing than his rider, especially in dim light. The horse is more active at night and has a huge range of vision. The horse can see about 340 of the 360 degrees around itself, with only two small blind spots, immediately in front of and directly behind it. Because the eyes are set on either side of the head, the horse does not see objects in depth. It sees them flat, as you or I would see if we shut one eye. The horse sees less detail than we do, but is more sensitive to movement. Despite its predominately lateral vision, the horse is capable of seeing a narrow band in three-dimensions if it directs its gaze forward. But because of the length of the nose and muzzle, this vision only works at a distance of about six feet out in front. This is important to remember. As a horse approaches objects it clearly sees with both eyes, the object disappears at the last minute, blocked by its own head. At this point the horse is navigating by instruments, so to speak. Or better yet, its rider.

It has also been thought that horses are color-blind. We now know that this is not the case; however, their color vision is much weaker than ours. The distance a horse can see is still up for argument; it has been documented that a horse can recognize its owner from dis-

A large eye allows better vision.

tances of up to a quarter-mile. Whether this is purely by visual recognition or identifying the owner's mannerisms, both require vision.

A large, open eye can see well all the way around. A horse with an eye set too far into the socket or small in size will not have the same peripheral vision as the horse with a large, open eye. A larger sight range results in a horse that is calmer, less spooky, and one that seems to be more sensible. This will make your job of getting him used to other environments besides home easier. Eyes set widely apart will also allow for better vision behind the horse, increasing his awareness of his rider. If a horse has a lot of white over the top of his eye, it usually means that his eye is a little bit smaller around. He is going to have a harder time with the field of vision in front and to his rear, increasing odds he'll be more flighty and/or spooky. An eye of larger diameter placed properly on corners of the head obviously provides better peripheral vision. When evaluating the eye, look for size, shape, and symmetry. I rate the eye an 8 because it is the organ allowing constant awareness of the surrounding environment of the champion barrel horse.

8—The Hindquarters: The powerhouse of biomechanical energy

The hindquarters are your energy powerhouse. I liken them to an engine. Ideally, the hindquarters should be at least 30 percent of the length of the overall horse. They should match the shoulder in angle and length. Inefficient length here will reduce speed, stamina, power, and ability.

When a horse is correct in his hindquarters and hind legs, you can draw a plumb line from the point of his hip down that intersects with the point of his hock and his fetlock straight to the ground. This represents proper angulations in relationship to all the bones in the hindquarters. If any deviation is acceptable here, it would be a horse that is slightly camped under. This makes it easier for a horse to get his hind leg up under himself when turning or stopping. A camped out horse wastes energy and has a reduced efficiency of stride. He also has a difficult time engaging the back and hip.

A short cannon bone is what you want, as in the front leg. There is no mechanical advantage to having a long cannon bone. Again it is a short lever, and science tells us short levers are just as efficient.

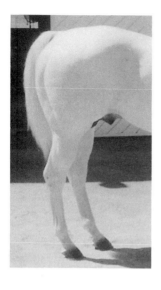

The size of the hock joint should support the size of the horse. Muscles and tendons pass over the hock for power and speed, so a larger joint will support better and absorb concussion while diffusing the horse's load. The inside and outside gaskin muscles should be correspondly large, helping the horse with lateral control and movement.

Further up is the stifle area, which should have a sloping and thick look to it from the front to the back. It should look like an upside down triangle, the widest part at the top, ending at a point at the bottom of the gaskin. This indicates a very strong stifle and will allow for stability.

The muscle running down the back of the rump along both sides of the tail needs to be long and tie in low, down by the hock. This will help the hind leg step way up under the horse. When walking, the hind foot will land in the tracks of the front foot. This will allow the horse to run fast and stop hard.

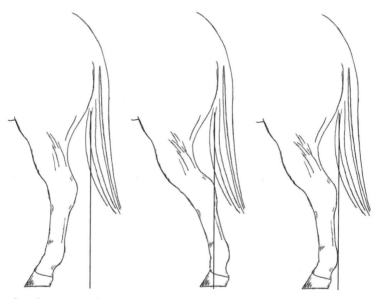

Camped under too much.   Camped out too much.   Perfect.

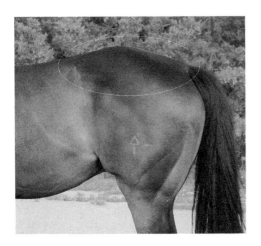

The croup should be long and slightly sloped.

Looking at the horse from behind, the leg bones and angles should again line up, as in the front legs. The bones should be centered and balanced, with centered joints. Excessive deviation could be detrimental in longevity and performance.

Now let's consider the croup. You want a good slope to the croup; how the pelvis is attached to the hip joint determines the length of stride of the hind limb. Slope gives the horse a quick, powerful start. This horse gets a hold of the ground much quicker than a horse that is flat through his croup.

I want to stress that rarely does a horse break down in muscle, but he breaks down in bone first and then that affects muscles. You need muscle for fast pushing and fast starts, but you must first have balanced structure to make them effective. The hindquarters are the powerhouse of biomechanical energy in any champion barrel horse.

7—The Withers: The lever used by the back muscles

The withers are an important attachment for the ligaments and muscles that extend the head, neck, shoulder, and back and are also the insertion point for muscles that open the ribs for breathing. Low, flat withers decrease range of motion and affect a horse's ability to collect. Withers provide a lever for the muscles of the back and neck to work together efficiently. When the head and neck lower or raise and extend, the back and loin muscles shorten and lengthen correspondingly.

Withers that are too low can cause problems with saddle fit. They are the pedestal for your saddle, and if they are too low, you will need to overtighten your cinch to keep your saddle in place, restricting a horse's ability to expand his lungs to get all the air needed to run fast.

Withers should be prominent and extend as far into the back as possible.

The withers need to extend far into the back, and this goes hand in hand with length of stride. Such conformation requires that the scapula, or shoulder bone, be longer. Remember, a long shoulder brings run in a horse. Also, look for overall smoothness and balance, including the way the neck and shoulder tie into the withers.

6—The Back and Underline: The gears of the hindquarters of the champion barrel horse

A horse's ability to engage depends on its ability to elevate the back and loins. This requires strong back and abdominal muscles. The proper length of the back should be less than one-third the overall length of the horse from peak of the withers to peak of the croup. A long back is flexible, but makes it hard to straighten, collect, or control the hind-quarters, which are required for speed as the loins are coiled to collect and engage the hindquarters, thrusting the rear limbs forward. It is also difficult to develop the muscle strength of a long back. The long-backed horse is more prone to fatigue, soreness, and crossfiring at the lope or gallop. A short back is best for speed, agility, quick directional

The Money Roll has an extremely long underline that has strong abdominal muscles.

changes, and control of the hindquarters. The short-backed horse seems to have fewer problems with sore backs.

We also want this horse to have good depth of his back, or heart girth, measured from the lowest point of the back, usually right behind the withers, to the bottom of the abdomen. Good depth here indicates strong abdominal muscles essential to strength and speed. Strong abdominal muscles go hand and hand with a strong back.

Along with the importance of the shorter backed horse, is the necessity of a long underline, measured from behind the elbow to the flank. The underline should be at least three inches longer than the back. A short back requires strong abdominal muscles; a long underline allows a horse to develop the abdominal muscles which work hard during hindquarter engagement. A long underline also keeps the horse from forging, or overreaching, when the hind leg reaches forward and interferes with a front foot. A horse with a short back and a short underline typically has more problems with interference.

5—Rib Shape and Depth: The house of the lungs

A wide chest and deep, well-sprung rib cage allows for full lung expansion during exercise. The heart girth area houses the lungs. Additionally, the heart, liver, and stomach are also protected within the confines of the rib cage. A large, well-sprung rib cage promotes full intake of air, which improves performance and muscular efficiency. The widest point of the rib cage should be right behind the girth area. Correct chest depth and rib capacity allow plenty of room for the legs, shoulder, and neck to attach, which in turn facilitates the range of motion we seek, muscular contraction, and speed of stride. It is a good representation of the size of the lungs and their capacity. The best way to tell if your horse has a deep heart girth is to put your saddle on and see how he cinches. I like a horse that takes a 32" or 34" cinch length and has 10 inches of latigo on each side when tightened to competition tightness.

5—Muzzle: Key to breathing and bit sensitivity

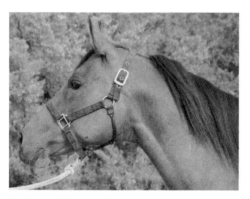

A short, thin muzzle.

I like a short, thin muzzle. The muzzle needs to be short so that the bit will be more effective. A short muzzle allows the bit to sit at the lowest point of the horse's head. Furthermore, a thin muzzle will make a horse more sensitive to the bit's pressure as it sits in the corners of his mouth. That will help when transmitting signals from your hands to the bit and to the horse's mouth. When the muzzle is short and thin, nostril expansion is easier, allowing proper oxygenation of the blood. Blood oxygenation again is crucial to enhanced performance and protects all of the horse's working parts. I rate the muzzle a 5 because of bit position, air intake, and sensitivity of the champion barrel horse.

4—The Head: Where air and nutrition enter
the champion barrel horse

Ideally I like a relatively short, broad head, short from muzzle to poll, wide between the eyes and nasal passages. A relatively broad forehead or face allows more room for air exchange through the air passages, as well as a large surface area for the facial muscles that open the nostrils for airflow. This area is also important for providing ample room for the horse's oral cavity and his teeth. A broad forehead often corresponds to width between the jaw bones, allowing freedom of movement of the throat and a wider passage area for air, blood, and food.

This horse has a beautiful head.

A dramatically dished face may limit air flow, contributing to poor endurance. However, a slightly dished or flat face provides the horse the maximum visual field possible. A bulging roman nose hinders the horse's ability to see in 180 degree arcs and may impinge on his already limited frontal field of vision. A long head hangs heavily on the end of the neck, perhaps at the cost of balance. Don't assess the head merely in terms of what's appealing to you, but what appeals to the form to function principles. The horse's head plays an important role in vision and the exchange of food, blood, and air in our champion barrel horse.

2—Ears: The signal flags of the champion barrel horse.

Believe it or not, hearing plays a huge role in a horse's performance. A horse's highly sensitive ears can detect a wide range of sounds, from very low frequency to very high. At nearly all levels equine hearing is more acute than human. Humans have the ability to hear 20,000 cycles per second, while a horse can hear up to 25,000 cycles per second. This declines with age just as it does in humans. Because they do not hear tones at the low frequency, like humans do, it is important to speak up when cuing and use higher pitches.

The horse's acuity of hearing is thanks to the large and mobile nature of the ear, which is controlled by sixteen muscles and can be rotated, independently if desired, about 180 degrees to pinpoint the source of sound from a great distance. Horses are able to listen

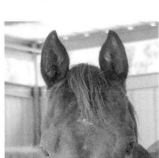

I like the ears on this horse. They are small and set on his head so they can move easily in any direction.

to their own movement, as well as voice commands, which are important when cuing your horse, especially in competition situations. The roar of the crowd, the booming voice of the announcer, or the rumbling engine of a tractor are frequently present while competing. Many sounds we ignore can be very irritating to a horse's highly sensitive ears. The movement of your horse's ears tells you exactly what he is concentrating on. The ears are truly organs of expression. Their ability to indicate both attention and annoyance helps the rider understand the horse's signals.

When assessing the ears, be sure they are set on his head so that he can move them forward and back freely. If a horse's ears are thick and set low on his head, he will not use them to better his performance. Watching a horse's ears move when you're riding him or watching him in a video, look for those ears to go forward and backward to indicate he's paying attention to where he is and what you're asking of him. The ear signals expression, direction, attention, and concentration of the champion barrel horse.

Ears show you expression.

Conclusion

Although I can draw and describe the perfect horse, finding him is nearly impossible. Look for the horse that most closely resembles the ideally conformed horse. Balance and proportion are key. If you are out shopping for a new horse, this chapter should help you find a horse that can run barrels easily.

If you already have a horse, consider his conformation and how it relates to his ability to compete. This new understanding will help you plan for your horse's strong points and his weaknesses.

Evaluate Movement

Perhaps by now you've found your prospective champion. You've considered pedigree and understand which conformation traits enhance form to function. Let's now talk about evaluating him in motion and/or under saddle.

When evaluating athletic movement, keep four points in mind: length of stride, rhythm, lightness of movement, and impulsion. The *length of stride* is the distance the horse will travel from the time one foot hits the ground until the same foot hits the ground again.

Rhythm refers to the patterns of footfall among the various gaits and how well the movement of each foot is in balance and in time with the others. Horses that have rhythm are capable of adjusting their stride, completing changes of direction and athletic feats more efficiently.

Lightness is the coordination of stride and rhythm so that movement appears to take minimum effort. It is the ease and efficiency with which the horse moves. The lighter the contact of hooves with the ground, the more efficiently a horse moves. This is the factor that assists in soundness and longevity because of reduced hoof and limb stress.

Impulsion is the effective use of the hindquarters to provide momentum, the force contributing to the length of stride, lightness, and rhythm which propel the horse forward. A horse with good impulsion drives off his hocks and moves forward with an elevated front end. The greater the impulsion, the longer the stride due to a longer suspension phase of that stride.

Ideally we'd like to evaluate a prospect, even one not yet under saddle, in a round pen or arena and watch him move without a rider. It is best to assess athletic movement at a strong or extended trot, so the horse can carry his head in a natural way. The trot is best because it is the only even two-beat gait. Keep an open mind and really evaluate this horse. Assess his balance and smoothness in both appearance and movement. Without a rider, he should handle himself with ease and freedom. When he changes gaits or stops and turns, he should naturally use his body well. These are the horses that can make necessary adjustments during performance. Conformation that is balanced and smooth in appearance will represent itself when he is moving.

Look for efficient forward movement: good reach with the front feet and very little upward knee action. We want a horse that barely lifts his feet off the ground before setting them down. If his conformation is good through the shoulder angle and down the front leg, this will be the case. His movement should be fluid and have length to it, with smooth motion over his back, loin, and hip, too. Think of this trait as gliding over the ground. He needs to present himself in a manner that makes you think he'd be smooth to ride.

Pay close attention to his head. Any deviation or bobbing while moving at the trot can indicate a soundness issue. Because the head goes up when a horse tries to minimize impact on a foot, pay close attention to this.

Ask the seller questions about his maintenance program, including vaccinations, worming, shoeing, and about past injuries. We want to be sure this individual has been well cared for. Many issues can be managed. If you find a tremendous individual with some small issues that can be improved upon, he is still worth evaluating.

For young horses, maintenance is important. Trimming their feet when they are babies can impact an entire career, as can proper nutrition. Be specific with the seller about care of young horses. You want to buy from a seller who has the proper knowledge of taking care of these potential athletes.

While you're watching this horse move around, don't let a long, flowing mane and tail or slick, shiny coat win you. Yes, they are indicators of good health and proper care, but they can also allow us to overlook serious flaws. A pretty color and a long tail and mane will surely be appealing, but focus on the areas we've discussed that will make or break this horse's potential success as a barrel horse. Double-check to be sure he has the traits that will allow him to succeed and enjoy the job of barrel racing. An athletic horse will move effortlessly because of a combination of length of stride, rhythm, lightness, and impulsion.

If you're watching a horse under saddle and rider, assess his training. Being broke doesn't mean he won't buck. Being broke means he has the proper foundation in training. He should respond to any commands immediately and willingly without resistance. He should give to the rider and bit; he should not throw his head up or shake it when asked to stop and turn around. He should be flexible and collect himself when asked to stop. He should know his leads well. These are all important areas required of a well-broke horse.

If you ride the horse, determine if he is a tight or loose moving horse. A tight horse is aware of himself and every muscle he has. It is easy to determine where these types of horses are going and what they are doing. A loose-moving horse will feel like you cannot tell where he is going next. It is hard to anticipate these kinds of horses, especially at speed.

Marlene and Dutch with Charmayne James and Scamper. These were the two best barrel horses in the 80s.

A well-broke horse has to do about five things really, really well. It's simple, but takes time to establish. We want him to stop, back up, roll back, flex or bend, counter-arc, and know his leads. He needs to be able to do these things at every gait and in both directions. When I ride, any move I make or ask for must be responded to immediately and in a positive way. This is the mark of a well-broke horse.

When you ride this horse, judge all of these things. Does he move off your legs well? When you ask him to stop is it right now? If this horse is stiff or grabs the bit when you ask him to stop, evaluate him for it.

It may be possible that you can make adjustments by adding a cavesson or tuning him up after you buy, but you must determine that for yourself. Ask yourself what you can deal with and what you can't, but know that a well-broke horse is absolutely required for successful, long-term barrel racing.

Heart and Disposition

Although the traits of heart and disposition are not easy to assess, they are an important aspect of an athlete.

The term "heart" refers to a horse's desire, determination, and grit. Barrel riders need a horse that wants to please us, is determined to please even in less than perfect circumstances, and is tough enough to handle the pressure of performance under any circumstance. These innate qualities are expressed through a horse's disposition. Although disposition is sometimes learned or accentuated by events or circumstances, aspects can be cultivated over time.

Don't confuse a horse that is aggressive and tough with an unruly horse. There is a difference between the horse that wants to kick your head off and the one that is athletically aggressive. Barrel horses need some aggressiveness to excel. Often the best horses for our event are not the easiest to be around; they may be quirky to handle on the ground. These individuals will almost always be stellar once you are aboard.

We don't want a horse that is dangerous, but we don't want one that is too passive either. Look for a horse that is kind *and* aggressive. And yes, a horse can be both.

Although it can't be scientifically proven, heart seems to be a genetic component. There are genetic crosses or combinations of bloodlines that over their history exhibit tremendous heart. Heart seems to also go hand in hand with pain tolerance. A big-hearted horse can cope with some pain and still perform. Now, we don't intentionally want our horses to work while hurt, but some tolerance here suggests this horse can perform even when the conditions are not perfect.

Disposition is one of the characteristics horses learn from their dams. A sour mare can influence the mental attitude of her colt. (This is another reason research on the dam is a plus.)

Horses, by their nature, are herd animals. They are either the leader or the follower. One animal in a herd dominates, and the rest of the band will look to this horse for leadership. Barrel racing horses need to be strong and exhibit leadership qualities to some extent, but at the same time be willing to submit to us as the leader when appropriate. Disposition is key to this characteristic.

If you are an experienced horseman, don't overlook a tremendous athlete simply because he is hard to catch or may pull back at the post when being saddled. All horses have their quirks. Understand your abilities and preferences. Some issues can be minimized with proper handling. If a horse pulls back, know you need to untie him before you cinch him up. If he is hard to catch, be creative in how you do it. Again, it is all a matter of what you are willing and able to work with.

Strong-willed horses statistically last longer and can handle the enormous stress and pressure we put on them when competing and hauling. When we look at great performance horses throughout history, we see that many of the best had their little quirks, but strong will and grit are ultimately what allowed them to overcome injury, illness, and challenges to become great.

CHAPTER 4

Champion Exam

*He who asks is a fool for five minutes, but he who
does not ask remains a fool forever.*

—CHINESE PROVERB

THE FINAL STEP in deciding whether to purchase a champion
prospect is the prepurchase exam. You are satisfied with the evaluation and selection process and need to have the picture completed by a professional. We need our veterinarians agreement that
our purchase is a sound one.

Buying a horse is a big investment; in most circumstances there are
no guarantees or refunds. This is why it is so important to investigate
every aspect of a horse before you buy. Only an accomplished veterinarian can determine the prospect's overall health, condition, and
soundness.

It doesn't matter whether you are buying a family horse, a horse to
trail ride, or a high performance athlete; your best chances for success
and happiness depend on the prepurchase exam. Any expense you
incur here will be well worth it, especially when you consider the long-term costs of keeping and caring for an individual with problems.

When buying a horse, arrangements are often made between the
buyer and seller regarding the prepurchase exam. When buying
a horse, the seller may agree to pay for the exam if they have misrepresented the horse in any way once the exam is complete. In the

same respect, if everything checks out okay whether you purchase the horse or not, you will generally pay for the exam. Either way, these are details that should be discussed between the buyer and seller before the exam occurs.

The information that can be obtained from the prepurchase exam is very valuable. If you avoid the purchase of a horse that is diseased or crippled, you will not only save yourself disappointment, but also money down the road.

The first step is finding an equine veterinarian. You may be looking at a horse in an area outside your hometown. In these circumstances, ask your hometown vet to recommend a vet in the area

Dr. Marvin Beeman DVM and I have a rapport that has developed over the past forty years.

you will be in. If this fails and you must use the seller's vet, you can always have x-rays and other test results forwarded to your vet to confirm the findings.

Make sure the vet you use to assist you is familiar with the breed, sport, or use this horse is intended for. Explain to the vet your expectations for this horse so he knows how the horse will be used. Let him know about your short- and long-term goals. A horse that is adequate for pleasure riding on trails may not hold up under high performance pressures.

Also be sure that you are giving the vet the opportunity to fairly evaluate the horse. The animal in question should be fit, conditioned, and in training for what you intend to use it for. A horse that has been laid off for an extended period of time will be difficult to evaluate for lameness. After an exam in such cases, you may request that the horse be returned to training and then reexamined after thirty days. Depending on the horse's value, such a request may be reasonable. You are, however, taking a chance that the horse will be sold between now and then.

Prepurchase exams can vary greatly. Deciding exactly what should be included in the purchase exam requires good communication between the seller, buyer, and vet. The value of the horse should also play a role in these decisions. If the investment is substantial, then a more thorough exam is recommended. If the value of the horse in question is minimal, it would not make sense to expend more than its value in exams.

By discussing the particulars and procedures of the exam process and why the vet recommends them, you are on your way to the actual process itself.

There is no standard for the procedures that are conducted during prepurchase exams. You and your vet must determine which tests are important for your needs.

The horse's medical history, including vaccinations, worming, shoeing, teeth care, supplements, drugs used, and so on are usually part of the process. Hopefully the seller will provide you with this information. The vet should obtain answers about any past or present difficulties. He may also inquire about the horse's work and exercise program. This information will all come from the owner or agent.

The next general area looked at will be the horses vitals—pulse, respiration, and body temperature. A blood sample should be taken to check

Prepurchase exams require a team of people.

for EIA (coggins) if current test results are not available. The vet will listen to the heart and lungs and also check the ears, nostrils, eyes, mouth, and teeth.

The next evaluation is for lameness. Traditionally, lameness has been defined as any alteration of the horse's gait. In addition, lameness can manifest itself in a change of the horse's attitude and performance. Abnormalities in performance and attitude can be caused by pain

Dr. Beeman using hoof testers to identify any possible unsoundness in the hoof.

most likely originating in the back, loin, hips, legs, or feet. Eighty percent of all lameness is discovered from the knees or hocks down, and 75 percent of that originates within the feet.

During a prepurchase lameness exam, the vet will try to determine two things. First, is the horse lame at the present time? Are there existing conditions that should be looked at more closely? Second, is this horse suitable for your needs? Factors include age, health, level of activity, conformation, and past use. The vet will evaluate body conformation, balance, and weight bearing and check legs for signs of past injury, stress, or disease.

An exam of the feet, both visual and with hoof testers, should identify any issues. A hoof testing instrument allows the vet to apply pressure to the soles of the feet to check for undue sensitivity or pain. He should palpate the horse, checking muscles, joints, bones, and tendons for evidence of pain, heat, swelling, or physical abnormalities.

At this point, the vet normally will evaluate the horse in motion in a straight line and in small circles. The horse should be observed on both hard and soft surfaces, since different types of lameness present under different footing conditions. The trot is the most useful of the gaits for evaluating lameness. It consists of a two-beat stride pattern, where the horse's weight is evenly distributed between

Evaluating a horse on a hard surface is very helpful in identifying lameness.

diagonal pairs of legs. In some cases, however, lameness may only be apparent during the faster gaits.

The vet should note deviations in gait, such as paddling or winging, failure to land squarely on all four feet, and the unnatural shifting of weight from one limb to another. He should look for and note shortness of stride, irregular hoof placement, head bobbing, stiffness, or shifting of weight.

A very important aspect in determining soundness is a range of flexion tests. The joints are flexed and held in place for a 60- or 90-second count; then the horse will be moved out at a trot to identify stiffness or soreness issues within the joints. Flexion can be done at any joint junction.

Radiographs are often included in prepurchase exams, but they are no substitute for a thorough, systematic exam. X-rays can give you a picture of how things are at the time that you buy the horse, but they cannot be used to predict the future. X-rays can also confuse the viewer by either providing a false sense of security or by suggesting problems that may never surface. Rely on a trusted vet's judgment regarding the need for x-rays.

Flexing the hock joint.

If further diagnostics are warranted, radiographs can be used to identify damage or changes that have occurred in the bony tissues. They can only be interpreted by an experienced and knowledgeable vet, because not all changes are of a big concern. A radiograph only provides limited information about soft tissues like tendons, ligaments, or structures inside the joints.

During a prepurchase exam for lameness, it is important to remember that even a favorable report is no guarantee. Because many factors affect a horse's ability in the short- and long-term, it is impossible to predict performance. Some of the factors of the lameness equation can include: conformation; hoof care; proper use of protective leg gear; saddle fit; daily exercise and conditioning; degree and manner of training; type and level of performance; age, skill, and experience of the rider; type and condition of the footing; disease and injury; and genetic predisposition.

The vet will also evaluate the horse's behavior, but at this point you've already considered this aspect during your own assessment.

If the horse is going to be used for high performance, a close inspection of the upper airways is recommended, using a treadmill and scope. Let your vet assist you with how detailed this type of test becomes.

Reproductive exams are also in order for stallions or mares. If you are considering a stallion, reproductive tests for libido and fertility are also warranted. Semen collection can be used to evaluate sperm counts, motility, and viability.

A mare should undergo rectal palpation to evaluate the reproductive tract for normal activity and structure. Additional tests such as ultrasound and uterine biopsy and cultures can help determine the health of her uterus and ability to conceive and carry a foal to term.

Site preparation before any injections are administered is very important.

A thorough clinical exam should alert you and the veterinarian to any problems. If anything is suspect during the basic tests, additional tests may be required, including more blood and urine panels to detect the presence of drugs that may affect exam results; additional x-rays or ultrasound exams; endoscopy or arthroscopy exams; nuclear scanning; nerve blocks; and blood, joint, fluid, and tissue samples. Such tests can be used to confirm a diagnosis or provide a clearer picture of the degree or seriousness of any problems discovered.

Diagnostic, nerve, and joint blocks are analgesic techniques useful for isolating a problem. The vet will systematically anesthetize specific segments of the limb one joint at a time until the lameness disappears, thus pinpointing the problem area. This procedure can also determine if a condition is treatable.

Nuclear scanning or scintigraphy is a procedure where dye is intravenously injected into the horse. The dye will concentrate in the area of the injury, which is scanned with a gamma camera to provide a reliable image of the area.

Ultrasound, or sonogram, uses sound waves to image internal structures.

Arthroscopy, or endoscopy, is a surgical procedure that allows visual examination of the inside of a joint or tendon sheath. It requires general anesthesia, and is sometimes the only way to diagnosis certain problems.

Blood, synovial (joint) fluid, and tissue samples can be examined for infection and/or inflammation. These tests usually require laboratory testing, which takes time.

Any additional exams and procedures must of course be cost effective in comparison to the value of the horse in question.

The American Association of Equine Practitioners has established a lameness grading scale, the scale ranges from 0 to 5, 0 being no lameness present under any circumstances and 5 being minimal weight bearing in motion or at rest with the possibility that an inability to move is present.

The next factor to consider in the prepurchase exam process is the cost of the exam. Again, you must look at the horse's value and believe this is an investment. If you plan on getting insurance on this horse, this exam and its outcome will be crucial to that process as well. Ask what costs will be associated with these procedures. If you are serious about a prospect, you can't afford not to get a thorough exam.

Make sure that you are present during the exam. Also require that the owner or agent be present. After the exam, discuss the results with the vet in private without the seller. Don't be afraid to ask lots of questions regarding the findings or for further information about them.

You should also understand that the vet doing the exam is not supposed to pass or fail a horse. Rather his job is to provide you with information regarding any existing medical problems, as well as discuss them so that you can make an informed decision in the purchase. Again, the vet can only advise you about the horse's condition. These areas should include conformation, eyes and vital organs, and most importantly his limbs for signs of disease or injury. The vet should be able to tell you how any issues might affect future performance from a health standpoint. But remember, future performance can't be predicted.

A thorough understanding of your vet's findings will help you make an informed decision about a prospective purchase. If you don't understand what your vet is telling you, by all means ask for clarification. When you discuss the results, remember that no horse is perfect, ever. Some conditions and faults are manageable or may never affect performance. If managing a condition or fault requires specialized shoeing, exercise, nutrition, medication, or care, make sure you can afford it and it is practical for your specific situation. If you doubt any aspect of the exam, get a second opinion. Finally, make your own decision whether the horse is a sound investment. The vet can't say if you are going to like riding the horse, if you can get along with it, or if you will win on it.

Remember you have to take an active role in this horse's condition. Understand the results of the tests. Ask lots of questions. Then add the findings to the other pieces of this "horse puzzle."

If helpful, make a list of positives and negatives about the horse, then weigh the results. When the prepurchase exam is complete, you should be able to make a very informed and wise decision on your prospective investment.

Insurance

Perhaps by now you have yourself a champion horse. Let's talk about insuring your investment.

Nobody likes to ever think about the potential of a tragedy occurring, but the potential is real. Horses seem to be prone to illness, accidents, and especially injury. In the case that a tragedy does occur it is nice to know that your investment is protected financially.

There are lots of companies that offer policies to protect horse owners from financial losses in the case of death and loss of use because of an accident, injury, and even theft.

Insurance is very specialized, and although I can give you some information about it, talk to your agent in depth about it.

Understand the terms and conditions of each coverage and the terms in which it applies. Believe me, there is more to it than buying a policy, making a claim, and collecting. You must educate yourself and do your part.

An insurance policy is a legal contract between you and the insurer. Read the contract closely. Ask for an explanation of terminology, phrases, words, and any provisions which you don't fully understand.

Know your responsibilities. If your horse gets hurt or has to be put down, know what specifics must be adhered to for the policy to be in effect. Know what guidelines are required in emergency situations, and don't wait until a crisis occurs to try and determine how your coverage applies.

Read all the print—yes, that means the fine print, especially! Know what phone numbers to call in the event something happens. Highlight them for quick access in case you need them. Keep the numbers in the barn and add them to your speed dial and cell phone. Most importantly, keep a copy with your travel papers in your truck or trailer. Most accidents occur away from home. The information in that policy will not help you if it is tucked away neatly in your office drawer 1,000 miles away.

Know what steps have to be taken if euthanasia is required. Many policies insist upon a second opinion in order for euthanasia to be implemented. In order for a claim to be valid, certain conditions must be adhered to depending on policy language and terms. The same applies for surgical policies. If your horse has colic, your insurance company must okay it in order for it to be covered. You can't just make the decision to put your horse down and expect the insurance company to pay you off.

Your agent can explain how to obtain the proper coverage that meet your needs. Agents also explain each policy's terms, conditions, and requirements for action from you, your veterinarian, and the company itself.

The basic types of insurance are mortality, loss of use, major medical, surgical, breeding infertility, theft, and specific perils.

Mortality Insurance will pay you if your horse dies, and an autopsy may be required. In the case of euthanasia, the intentional destruction of a horse for humane reasons, most companies require advance notification and prior permission, except in the most extreme cases. The insurance company may require a second opinion. Euthanasia must be based solely on medical considerations, not economic ones, regardless of age, value, or sex.

Four criteria are given by the American Association of Equine Practitioners to help you make this determination:

First—Is the condition chronic and incurable?
Second—Does the immediate condition have a hopeless prognosis for life?
Third—Is the horse a hazard to himself or his handlers?
Fourth—Will the horse require continuous medication for pain relief for the remainder of his life?

Loss of Use Insurance is paid on a percentage basis if the horse is permanently incapacitated for its intended use or purpose. This coverage usually costs double the normal amount and is quite hard to get. If you purchase this type of insurance, again understand its conditions. Keep good records of income, winnings, and earnings generated by your horse to prove what loss of use means to you.

Major Medical is like health insurance. It offsets major catastrophic veterinary care. This covers specific procedures, such as colic, and most trips to the vet related to an injury. Again read the terms. Don't just assume surgical protection means any surgical procedure, only to find out your horse's surgery bill is not covered.

Breeding Infertility policies cover stallions and mares against reproductive failure.

Specified Peril Insurance covers situations like lightning, tornados, fires, transport injury, and theft. Generally each must be specified, however, so make sure you understand your coverage by asking the person selling the policy. Keep all your records and correspondence between yourself and the agent and company in case any discrepancies in coverage arise.

• • •

SOME OTHER considerations regarding insurance should be remembered. Know the time period you have to report any health problems to your insurance company. Determine and know how to get prior approval for surgeries. Know what documentation is required when submitting a claim, such as required medical documents from your vet. Know if your horse is covered when you're traveling out of state or with another party. Have your vet document on the application for insurance and the original health exam documents what you use the horse for. Understand your financial obligations for exams, lab tests, and other procedures not covered by insurance. Know the exact value of your policy and how it will be paid out under different circumstances. For instance, in a loss of use case, your horse will have a salvage value that will be deducted versus a complete loss in a mortality case.

The better covered your horse is and the better prepared you are, the less traumatic these experiences will be. Additionally, economic impact should be alleviated by insurance.

Because most equine insurers require a health exam, during a pre-purchase exam is a perfect time to get things in order to obtain coverage. Depending on what types of coverage you are getting, the exams required will vary.

Remember a vet can't attest to a horse being insurable. Your vet can only respond to the questions presented by the application for a policy. He must report the facts to the best of his ability, but has no role in determining if you will get coverage.

Regardless of the situation, never ask or expect a vet to file an insurance claim for you or to be an insurance expert in emergencies. It is your responsibility to be well-informed and well-educated where insurance is concerned.

You, your vet, and your insurance company all have a role in maintaining the integrity of the horse industry. Regardless of the coverage, the horse's welfare must always be at the forefront of any decision made on its behalf.

PART THREE

Champion Program

*An army of lions commanded by a deer
will never be an army of lions.*

—NAPOLEON BONAPARTE

CHAPTER 5

Champion Team

And if any one for as you to go one mile, go with him two miles.

—MATTHEW 3:41

WE HAVE our champion rider, and we have our champion horse. Let's complete our champion program puzzle with a group of professionals we can count on to keep this equine athlete performing at his best; the champion team.

The professional team should include a veterinarian, equine dentist, farrier, and various alternative resources to assist us with our finely tuned equine athlete.

Just as can be noted in the quote at the beginning of this chapter, if someone inspires us to seek out their help in poor circumstances, we should also seek out their assistance in good circumstances. Don't just rely on these people for tragedy or emergency; include them in your day-to-day program.

We all need to establish good communication and working relationships with our equine professionals before an emergency occurs. Think of how much easier it is to troubleshoot a problem with a trusted friend than it is with a stranger.

Over time, these professionals get to know their clients and patients. If they are working with our horses routinely, they establish a relationship with us and our horses and understand our personalities, expectations, and normal patterns and responses.

Our horses also get to know these professionals over time. If we have never visited a dentist and we have to have emergency oral surgery, we don't feel comfortable with a dental surgeon we don't know from Adam. We are more at ease however if this person is someone we know from being seen on a regular basis. Establishing relationships with your professional team puts you, the professional, and your horse at an advantage during treatment.

As you can see from the chapter on the prepurchase exam, a trusted and credentialed veterinarian is important to our team. Regardless of whether you need one immediately, it is imperative to get acquainted with a veterinarian who deals with clients in our sport, or at least clients with performance horses.

If you don't currently have a veterinarian, look for an equine clinic that is specifically geared toward performance horses. Although a regular farm veterinarian might do just fine administering vaccinations, worming, and preparing a Coggins test or Health Certificate, but when the time comes for serious problems, we need to have a specialist on our list.

By choosing a clinic that specializes in performance horses, we know we can have the best professionals at our disposal when needed. In clinic environments, there are several vets who see lots of horses daily. Your vet then has several colleagues to confer with when making decisions about treatment and diagnosis. As they say, "Two heads are better than one."

One or more of these partners will likely be a board-certified surgeon. A surgeon has completed several more years of training, which gives him an advantage when dealing with emergencies, lameness, and injury situations. A surgeon is well-versed in internal problems and damages that occur. He makes his living repairing broken bones, torn tissues, and acting quickly to save equine lives.

It is of the utmost importance that you are active in your horse's care. Learn how to take vital signs (heart rate, temperature, and respiration), give intramuscular or even intravenous shots, and so on. If you are 500 miles from home in an emergency, knowing how to act in these situations can save your horse's life while you are looking for a vet. If you are on the road and your horse has colic in the trailer, being able to administer Banamine IV can save his life. Work with your vet to be prepared. Express an interest in your horse's health care and well-being. You will find if you are diligent and well informed, your vet will enjoy you as a client and help you become a better horseman.

Our champion's performance relies on proper dental care. Routine dental care is essential to your horse's health. We need a trusted equine dentist on our team to make sure this champion can eat properly and has a well-cared-for mouth to carry the bit. We want him to be content. All of these factors can increase our horse's life span. Because of the important role dental care plays in both feed utilization and performance, I have dedicated a whole section to it in the Champion Care chapter.

We need a stellar farrier to be in control of our champion's hooves—his foundation. This being one of the most important pieces of champion performance, hoof maintenance also has its own section under Champion Care.

The final aspect of a professional team would be some accomplished alternative practitioners. Some examples of these would be an

Doug, Dutch, and I soaking his foot and waiting for an abscess to break. There are many trying times in the horse business.

equine acupuncturist or acupressure professional, an equine massage therapist, and a laser technician. The addition of acupuncture, chiropractics, massage therapy, and laser technology can keep your horse performing at his best or help him recover more rapidly from injuries and surgeries. These practices complement medical care and can be one of those critical pieces that make complete our puzzle.

Quite often, a performance problem or attitude issue can be resolved by corrective shoeing, dental care practices, or by alleviating another source of pain or discomfort. Remember, our horses can only express a problem through their actions and attitude. It is our job as responsible horsemen to know our horses, monitor changes in performance and attitude, and correct problems. An intelligent horseman is aware of his horse's unspoken words and needs at all times.

CHAPTER 6

Champion Care

Practice with a purpose, practice with a plan, practice with patience.

—JOSEPH PARENT

Facilities

ACILITIES for your horse can be as elaborate or simple as you'd like—or, in many cases, as you can afford. Your horse facilities will depend greatly on your personal needs and budget. The bare necessities are an outside pen area, some type of shelter for him, a feeding area, and a place to ride him. The most important thing is that the facilities are safe, functional, and well maintained.

There are as many ways to keep a horse as you can possibly imagine. A horse may be turned out in a lot, pasture, run, pen, or corral, or even stalled in a barn. Size is important. The bigger the area, the better for a horse. Horses do like to lie down, and if the area you choose for the major living area is small, he will not lie down as much as needed.

Your horse needs some sort of shelter, perhaps a loafing shed, lean-to, stall, or even simply a stand of trees. He needs a place to get out of the sun, wind, rain, and snow if he chooses. Some horses prefer to face these elements without shelter, but you'll probably sleep better if he has the option. Be aware shelter may be required by law. Check your state regulations.

Make sure you keep all your troughs and feeders well away from fencing to avoid the chance of your horse getting tangled in wire or boards while he is trying to eat. This is especially important if you feed more than one horse in the same pasture or area.

Sometimes people will use feedbags in multiple horse situations to feed one horse grain or supplements and not another. This is a dangerous practice in my opinion. Horses have been known to drown because an owner put on a feedbag and did not remove it promptly. If you are doing other chores or not paying attention, you could play a role in a horse's death because of it. It can happen to even the most diligent owner. Separating horses while feeding is best. If this is not possible or if there is no other option, tie them up to eat grain out of a bucket. Assuming that your horse is properly trained to tie, he will survive if you forget him, but he might not if you forget to remove a feedbag.

If you have a free standing feeder, make sure the base is narrower than the rim. Rubber feed pans, large tractor tires with plywood bottoms, and buckets are best. If you are feeding several horses, spread out their feed to avoid fighting, kicking, and injuries.

If you use hay racks or mangers, make sure they are at wither level or lower so horses don't hit their heads. Additionally, if racks are above the withers, horses must pull down their hay, and dust and hay particles fall into their nostrils and eyes. Equine dentists have also noticed that horses that have to reach up and pull hay have more problems with hooks on their teeth, which must be removed.

Although many people opt for hay nets made of nylon or rope, I don't recommend them. Yes, they are soft and horses don't normally injure themselves by bumping them, but you risk your horse getting a foot caught in them. They can be extremely dangerous because of this. Additionally, horses will often use them as a toy, chewing and pulling on them, which may pull the net down to foot-tangling level.

After feeding, horses are thirsty. Your horse needs to have access to fresh, clean water at all times. If you can't have running water or waterers that periodically freshen and oxygenate your horse's drinking water, add fresh water to your trough daily. Doing this will prevent it from becoming stale by adding oxygen to it.

If you have automatic waterers, make sure any new horses introduced to them know how to use them and are not afraid to drink from them.

If you must use buckets, use rubber ones. Although plastic buckets and containers are light and inexpensive, they become brittle and shatter from the elements. Make sure the bucket is larger at the top than the bottom as to allow the horse to get his nose into it without interfering with his eyes.

Periodically clean your troughs, buckets, and water containers by scrubbing and bleaching them. They get slimy quick. A good rule of thumb is to ask yourself if you'd mind drinking your horse's water. If you wouldn't dare, then you need to do some adjusting to provide better drinking conditions for your horse. A horse should have access to at least thirty gallons of water a day, depending on his level of exercise and the weather.

If you live in an area subject to freezing temperatures, you need to take necessary measures to prevent water from freezing; use a water heater or be diligent about breaking the ice that forms on top of it. If you use a water heater, make sure your horse can't chew on the cord. Take the necessary precautions to encourage your horse to drink ample amounts of water in cold weather.

The final thing we need is a place to ride. If you do not have a place to ride your horse on your property or nearby, locate one to haul or ride to. This is the only way you can condition your champion horse.

I actually prefer working my horses in a large, open area that I can groom with a tractor. What matters is that it is large enough and that the ground is well taken care of. Avoid working your horse on ground that is too hard or uneven, especially ground that has holes or large clods of compacted dirt. Very deep footing is hard on a horse, also. I like 6- to 8-inch depth.

Now let's talk about our facilities being safe. Check all your facilities on a daily basis for nails, splintered boards, or sharp, protruding edges. Horses can damage and change their surroundings quickly by rubbing, chewing, or by playing around with their neighbor. Be constantly aware of your horse's facilities, for safety's sake.

Check gate latches, chains, hooks, and fences. If all latches, chains, and fences are in good working order and placed so that horses can't chew on or play with them, we know the risk of dangerous escape will be minimized. So is potential liability.

Make sure your horse has adequate room, regardless of where you keep him. Avoid putting two horses in a long, narrow run. Two horses cannot move freely past each other this way. Their hips are precious, and in narrow confinement two horses may bump hips or run each other into the surrounding structure.

Don't keep your manure pile near your pens, which will increase flies and parasites around our horses. Locate your manure pile well away from your pens and shelter. Don't store feed and hay out in the open to bleach in the sun or become wet and moldy. An inexpensive tarp will protect hay if you don't have a hay barn, and a garbage container can keep grains dry and dust free. Choose metal bins with secure lids to avoid pest contamination.

Maintenance and cleanliness will keep any facility efficient and safe. Repair loose boards. Pick up wire and nails. Check that screws on your latches are tight. Remove manure daily from stalls and sheds. Sweep aisles and remove manure. Keep your tack clean, neat, and orderly. Replace bedding when necessary. Clean water troughs and feeders regularly. Remove leaves, debris, spiders, and cobwebs from interiors. Take the necessary steps to keep your facilities in the best condition possible. If your surroundings are well-kept, both you and your horse will be healthier and more comfortable while you chase your dreams.

● ● ●

★ CHAMPION NUTRITION ★

*Horse feed is a science, but
feeding horses is an art.*

—CARL NAFZGER,
TRAINER OF KENTUCKY DERBY CHAMPION, UNBRIDLED

I BELIEVE in good quality, clean, and fresh nutritional products. I suggest you contact your local feedstore and ask if they know of a good equine nutritionist that you could talk to. You will gain a great respect and knowledge for these people and learn about the different feeds available in your area. Know how much your horse weighs. Feeding amounts and medications are based on pounds or milligrams per hundred pounds of body weight. The program I have had success with throughout my career follows.

My rule of thumb is feed one and one-half pounds of hay per one hundred pounds of body weight per day. Each new load of hay will weigh more or less due to moisture content. I like to feed one daily feeding of 100 percent second cut alfalfa. Alfalfa is called the Queen of Forages; it has the highest feeding value of all commonly grown hay crops. Alfalfa is high in mineral content and contains at least ten different vitamins. Second cut hay grows with a fine stem that is palatable, with a protein content of 16 to 20 percent. The first cutting usually has more stem, due to the length of the growing season, and it will be lower in protein as well. If I cannot get second cutting, I will choose first rather than third of fourth. For my second daily feeding, I offer grass hay. There are several varieties; find one that is grown in your area. The protein content will vary depending on how much fertilizer was applied to the field to be harvested, normally between 7 to 9 percent, and different varieties of grass hays have various vitamins and minerals, if any at all. If you have a choice, here are my preferences, in order: timothy, brome, orchard, oat, or coastal. Feed the same amount in weight no matter what type of hay you use.

I feed the hay on clean, hard ground or in a low feed tub, to prevent dirt from entering the nasal passageways and possibly causing problems. With advances in equine dentistry, we now know that horses that are fed in higher feeders that cause the horse to pull his hay out have teeth that have a tendency to develop more hooks in the lower back quadrants. I have fed low to the ground for years without any problems. When I am away from home, I wet down the area to feed on if it is sandy or dusty. At home, you can put down a rubber mat or use a plastic barrel cut in half. Because the horse is a grazing animal, his esophagus is designed to function best when his head is lowered. If he can't lower his head to swallow, as might happen in a trailer, a life-threatening condition called "choke" may result.

I prefer Canadian or North Dakota–grown oats. I like them whole because, when rolled or crimped, oats will lose half the protein content in the following three to four months. If the oat kernel is not disturbed, it will hold its protein content for two years.

The amount of grain you feed depends on the age of the horse and the amount of daily work. An average amount of grain for a horse I ride every day is four pounds per day—a small amount compared to halter horses or racehorses. If you need more or less energy or weight, adjust by one pound either way until you get the results you want. Remember the quote at the beginning of this section; feeding is an art.

If you need to add some more weight to a horse or live in extreme cold weather areas, you can add barley to the oats for more energy. I feed two parts oats and one part barley in the winter. It is hard to beat a natural, good quality grain.

Offer a balanced diet. If for some reason you choose not to feed alfalfa, then you need to add a vitamin supplement along with the oats. You can choose to feed complete grain rations, combinations of grains, molasses, and vitamins formulated into a well-balanced ration. They come in various protein percentages, and you determine what your horse needs based on daily work. I do not like complete rations as well as oats, because of the unknown quality of grains that can be used.

The supplements I spoke of earlier meet certain needs of hard-working barrel horses. The first thing I recommend is a joint supplement that has been carefully formulated to help maintain healthy joints. I stress the word "formula," because my nutritionist has made me aware that it takes "this" to make "that" work, and so on. Do your homework and ask professional trainers what they are using and getting good results with. Beware of trainers that are being paid to use products; this will influence their opinion. I like to go into trainer's barns and look in the feed room to see exactly what is being used—with permission, of course.

The second supplement is a formula that I have used for twenty years. It consists of Vitamins A, D, and E, as well as corn, soybean, and wheat germ oils. This formula lubricates the lining of the intestine to help feed pass through easily to reduce risks of colic and to help prevent worm damage. Strong, pliable hooves and great hair coats make me believe that oiling from the inside out is the best way to healthy feet. I put four ounces per day on the grain every feeding year-round.

If I am not feeding alfalfa or I am buying hay on the road when I am away from home, I will feed a very balanced vitamin supplement, in the form of a small pellet or alfalfa-based crumble, a form I prefer over liquids or powders. Read labels and compare to decide what one will be best for your horse.

I offer my horses loose minerals at all times in a container, out of the weather, like in their stall or shed. Horses store minerals and will only eat them when they need them. Force-feeding minerals to horses can be damaging, unlike vitamins that will be passed through the system if not used. I prefer loose minerals over a block form because a horse's tongue is soft, and licking a hard mineral block may not be every horse's choice.

Water is critical to allow a horse to digest the large amounts of forage he eats a day. It takes one gallon of water to digest every one and one-half pound of hay. When I travel, I unload every five hours to allow a horse to drink. As soon as I get to an event, I unload and put water in front of my horse. If you offer a horse water throughout the day, they will never drink too much and get full and heavy with water.

Never feed your horse hay within six hours before you use this horse. The mechanics of digestion localize blood flow in the stomach and intestines during digestion. If we ask a horse to work hard during digestion, blood flow is limited to the legs and feet, increasing the chances of injury. After you eat, you do not feel like running or exercising, and horses are just like you. On this subject, the brain is not as sharp or quick right after you eat. I do not eat for four hours before I compete.

However, grain can be fed three hours before competition; the smaller quantity can be more quickly digested. It will also elevate blood sugar to a level that gives your horse more energy.

This picture of one of our horses shows the perfect weight for this individual. Notice how the hair coat, mane, and tail shine. You have to be the judge of your horse; the hair coat and feet condition will tell you if the feeding and worming programs you are using are working.

Deworming and Vaccinations

In order for our champion horse to be at his best, we must ensure that he is free from parasites and protected from disease. By being diligent and establishing a concrete worming and vaccination program, we can help our champion enjoy optimum health.

You want your horses to have a shiny hair coat, hooves without dry cracks, and good muscle definition.

Internal parasites, or worms as they are frequently called, silently diminish health and often contribute to the death of our beloved equine athlete. They cause extensive internal damage to organs, lower resistance to infection, rob our horse of nutrients, cause colic and poor health, and even produce a dull hair coat. Internal parasites are often overlooked thieves and killers.

More than 150 species of internal parasites affect our champion horse. The most common and troublesome are: large and small strongyles; roundworms or ascarids; tapeworms; lungworms; pinworms; bots; and threadworms. The first four are the most important in terms of healthcare.

The life cycle of most internal parasites involves three stages: egg, larva, and adult. Eggs or larvae are deposited onto the ground in the manure of an infected horse. They are then swallowed while the horse grazes or eats off the ground. The larvae become adults within the horse's digestive tract, specifically the stomach and intestines. Some species of parasites migrate out of the intestines into other tissues and organs before they return to the intestines to mature and lay eggs.

In the larvae stage, large strongyles will penetrate the lining of the bowels and migrate along the blood vessels that supply the intestines. Even in small numbers, they can cause extensive damage and even death.

A horse that is infected with large strongyles can appear unhealthy, lose weight, and develop anemia and colic. An infested young horse's growth and development will suffer. In most cases, colic caused by these pests will be relatively mild, but severe infections can result in loss of blood supply to the intestines, leading to the possibility of fatal colic.

Small strongyle larvae do not penetrate the intestinal wall or migrate to other organs. Instead, they burrow into the intestinal lining and remain dormant, or encysted, for several months before completing their life cycle. Unfortunately, during this time they are resistant to most dewormers. Therefore, they can cause severe damage to the lining of the intestine, especially when a large number of larvae emerge from the encysted stage at once. Colic and diarrhea are common in heavily infected horses. These parasites also cause weight loss, slowed growth in young horses, poor coat condition, and lack of energy. It is common for a horse's general health and performance to greatly improve after treatment for these particular parasites.

Before and after the small strongyle larvae burrow into the lining of the intestine, the parasite is susceptible to several dewormers. There are currently only two dewormers that are effective against the encysted larvae stage, which is when the most damage is caused. Strategic use of these two products is targeted at the encysted larvae and called "larvicidal" therapy.

Roundworms, or ascarids, are most often a problem in young horses, particularly foals, weanlings, and yearlings. Read the labels on the wormer you are using and make sure it kills ascarids. An adult roundworm can be several inches long and almost the width of a pencil. In large numbers, they can completely block, or impact, the intestine. Roundworm larvae can migrate through the internal organs until they reach the lungs, where they are coughed up and then swallowed back into the digestive tract to complete their cycle.

Infestation in young horses causes coughing, poor body condition and growth, a rough coat, pot belly, and colic. Colic is generally seen in heavily infested foals over three months old. Colic generally occurs after they are dewormed for the first time. By this time the roundworms may have matured into adults and the deworming causes impaction.

Tapeworms were not considered to be a significant problem in horses until recently. We now know they can cause colic as well, which may range from mild cramping to severe cramping requiring surgery. The life cycle of a tapeworm requires a small mite as an intermediate host. This mite is found in grass, hay, and grain. When a horse eats them, they are most susceptible to becoming infected. Recently, an equine dewormer called Praziquantel was approved to effectively fight the tapeworm. It is often found in combination with other products, such as ivermectin and moxidectin, which offer complete antiparasitic coverage. Deworm your horse for tapeworms annually.

There are other parasites of concern, such as lungworms. They cause chronic coughing in horses, ponies, and mules. The donkey is a natural host of this parasite, so typically they don't show any signs.

Pinworms lay eggs on the skin around the horse's anus. If you have a horse that constantly rubs its tail, it could be due to irritation caused by this parasite.

Bots do not usually cause major health problems, but they can cause damage to the stomach where they attach. Since ivermectin has become readily available, bots are rarely found in horses that are properly dewormed. The bot may also cause small areas of ulceration inside the mouth from burrowing larvae.

Threadworms are predominantly a problem in young foals and can cause diarrhea.

Contrary to popular belief, horses can have potentially dangerous numbers of parasites and appear to be healthy. In some individuals, especially young horses, parasites take a visible toll. Watch your athlete for any of these signs: dull, rough hair coat, decreased energy or depression, decreased stamina, loss of condition, slowed growth, pot belly, colic, and diarrhea.

How do you put these nasty critters out of business?

The fecal egg count is the most useful tool in controlling parasites. Collect one or two fresh manure balls and take them to your vet to be sent to a laboratory. This simple test identifies which parasites are present and the severity of the infestation. The results will be expressed in eggs per gram. A count of 200 suggests light infestation, while between 500 to 1,000 is high and suggests that the interval between your deworming is too long. You should perform these tests every six to twelve months.

Remember that a negative fecal exam does not mean your horse is free of parasites. Some parasites produce eggs intermittently, and larvae do not produce eggs at all.

Now we know the enemy, fight them. There are several dewormers on the market. Most are broad spectrum, meaning they rid the horse of several different types of parasite. I recommend you use a broad spectrum product as a base for your program. If you identify specific parasites like tapeworms or encysted small strongyles, add a specific wormer to the base program.

Remember that no program is 100 percent effective in ridding your horse of all parasites. However, reducing the parasites will improve your horse's health, minimize disease, improve feed efficiency, and reduce subsequent contamination.

If your horse is allowed grazing or pasture feeding, daily wormers can be worth your time. With such products, you feed a small amount of dewormer each day to prevent new infestations during grazing. However, they will not resolve existing infections or kill bots, so don't rely on them solely.

When a paste or liquid dewormer is used, establish the frequency based on your circumstances. In some cases, it may be best to deworm every thirty days, in others every two months. Have your vet help you determine the best interval for your program.

Whether you rotate your products is always controversial. When you use the same product for a long period of time, the parasite may become resistant to it. However, if you rotate too often, you may be creating strains of parasite that are resistant to several different products. Again discuss this with your vet.

There are three ways to administer dewormers: oral paste syringe, feed additive, and by stomach tube. All three of these methods are effective if you give the proper dose at the right time in the parasite cycle. Also make sure your horse receives the full dose. We have all had a horse spit dewormer out. Calculate your dose by weight of your horse. I give 100 pounds more to adjust for loss.

Although pastes and feed additives are convenient, some horses don't find them palatable, and they do spit them out. Again, make sure the entire required amount is consumed.

Tube worming via a stomach tube is highly effective because your horse will receive the proper dose. However, the range of commercial dewormers now available makes this veterinary process seldom necessary and cost prohibitive.

When you are creating a program, you have three options. They are continuous, interval, and strategic programs.

Of course the continuous program is based on feeding an additive daily throughout the entire year. Interval deworming is based on medication administered at regular intervals depending on your program. Strategic deworming is based on deworming at certain times of the year by fecal egg counts.

You can also use a combination of these. There is no single program that suits all horses or all situations. The ideal program depends on the number of horses you have, ages, management practices, and geographic location. Have your regular vet help you create of complete deworming program.

Because parasites are transferred mainly through manure, management is the key. Keep the number of horses per acre to a minimum to prevent overgrazing and reduce contamination. Pick up and dispose of manure regularly. Don't spread fresh manure on pastures or fields where horses are grazing. Mow and harrow pastures to break up manure piles. This also exposes larvae to the elements. Worms can't survive freezing, extreme heat, or drying out. Consider pasture rota-

VACCINATION SCHEDULE

DISEASE	COMPETITION HORSES	FAMILY HORSES
Tetanus Toxoid	Annually	Annually
Encephalomyelitis	Annually	Annually
EEE, WEE, VEE (sleeping sickness)	Annually	Annually
Rhino pneumonitis	Biannually	Annually
EHV-1 and EHV-4 (equine herpes virus)	Biannually	Annually
Strangles (equine distemper)	Annually (Intranasal)	Annually
West Nile	Biannually *(In February or March)*	Biannually *(In June or July)*
Influenza (flu/snotty nose)	Biannually	Annually *(Booster prior to likely exposure but only one more time a year)*

tion with sheep or cattle. This interrupts life cycles of equine parasites. Separate foals and weanlings from older horses to minimize exposure to adult horse parasites. Remove bot eggs regularly from hair. Time worming day so your horse has two days off afterward. I also separate worming and vaccinating days so I do not stress the immune system too much at once.

Establishing an effective parasite control program is as important as food and water to our champion horse, one more of the pieces we need in place to complete that champion puzzle.

Let's move on to our vaccination program. There are several key vaccinations our champion horse requires. Whether he is a future star or a veteran, there are specific vaccines which should be part of your program. Because vaccination schedules may vary widely depending on your horse's circumstances and where you live, develop a protocol with your vet.

It is important to know that a booster for tetanus should be given at the time of any penetrating wound or surgery, if the last dose given was not within the last six months. Use the antitoxin for injuries if there is no history of your horse being vaccinated with tetanus toxoid.

With sleeping sickness vaccines, give a booster every six months in endemic areas and prior to likely exposures, such as a county fair, clinic, or seminar, etc. Any time you take a horse to an environment shared with lots of other horses, discuss the need for additional vaccines or boosters with your vet.

For strangles there is a new intranasal product called "Pinnacle." It has proven to be very effective, unlike the injectable, which I do not recommend.

West Nile is 30 percent fatal in non-vaccinated horses. It can cause serious neurological problems, so make sure that you vaccinate twice, four to six weeks apart, the first time you give it. You should do this every March and July prior to your mosquito season.

Parasite control and vaccination programs are vital parts of the champion puzzle. With hard work and a desire to be dedicated to your horse's health, you will tailor a complete deworming and vaccination program to each individual horse and program. Once it is in place, you will see a whole new level of health, vitality and performance from your champion horse. Record keeping is of utmost importance. Keep a medical record book for every horse you own.

★ CHAMPION Shoeing ★
Shoeing + Common Sense = Healthy Horses
by Doug McRae

LIKE MOST horse care, properly shoeing a horse requires common sense. A horse's hoof must be balanced from side to side and front to back; the hoof must be level; the front two feet must match in toe length, angle, and size; and the back hooves must match each other without compromise. A horse needs traction to maintain footing while possessing precision to maintain soundness and health.

Common sense tells me that a horse's foot should be round. The front two feet should match in size, angle, and length, and they must be level. Ditto for the back two. It is not imperative that the front and back match other than in being level. This is the only way we can keep the horse's stride properly balanced without interference. Common sense.

Yes, every rule has exceptions, such as horses with bad conformation or major injuries. However, I will concentrate on rules regarding the good performance horses. As a whole, these horses are very similar in conformation and physical makeup. The better horses I have shod fall into a specific category regarding size, angle, length of toe, and levelness. Here is an overview of the averages that I have seen regarding these performance horses.

Shoe size is generally a size one in front and a size two behind. I never like to put a shoe on a performance horse smaller than a size one. Of course, these horses are usually four years old and up. I have never run across a horse this age with a foot this small. On the other hand, I have placed quite a few size two shoes on the front of performance Quarter Horses with excellent results. The size of the shoe directly affects soundness maintenance in regard to hoof growth, heel growth, and support for all joints in the leg. The larger shoe behind contributes more support at the back of the hind foot for additional stability as he uses his hind legs underneath his body.

The angle of heel generally runs in the 50 degree to 55 degree range. Any less or any more is a result of trimming too much heel and not paying attention to toe length. Specifically I have found an angle of 52 to 54 degrees in the front and 50 to 52 degrees behind as the goal to shoot for.

The ideal length of toe is $3\frac{3}{8}$ inches on the front feet and $3\frac{1}{2}$ inches on the back feet. I would rather shoe every five weeks and leave a little more hoof than shoe every six to seven weeks, going too short each shoeing. Be careful.

"Level? Are you kidding, my farrier is so good he can eyeball whether my horse is level or not! How do I know he is this good? He tells me so!" Not good enough for me and my horses. Especially when shoeing to be the best in the world, it is imperative that a level gauge is used.

This is a horse's front foot six weeks after being shod. Notice how the hoof is growing over the shoe. This is not acceptable, as it destroys the hoof wall and collapses the heels. This is a case of too small a shoe being applied.

Shoe Types

A barrel racer's shoe job can be the difference between success and failure, perhaps more than any other factor.

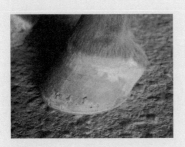

Here are some suggestions you might pass on to the farrier who shoes your barrel horse. The type of shoe that I presently use is the St. Croix Rim Lite. These shoes have all of the features that I look for; they wear well, are rigid to prevent hoof wall separation and damage, and are readily available. Occasionally I have used polo plates, but I have found that they are too thin and have a tendency to flex and bend out of shape, causing hoof wall separation. If you insist on polo plates, I suggest re-shoeing every four weeks to help eliminate hoof damage from the before-mentioned flexing. Shoeing this often will require a very proficient farrier, or you may experience more harm than good.

Here is a representation of the "all new" way of thinking about shoeing, The Natural Balance Method. There may be some validity to these methods. However, if the hoof is not level, balanced, and supported by a large enough shoe, the shoe type is the least of the owners worries. This photo shows the farrier's goal must have been to contract the heel area. Much too tight a fit.

Compare the bare foot here to the shod foot opposite. Notice the foot is not shaped liked the shoe that was applied. That cannot be healthy, can it? This foot is now ready to have the shoe shaped and applied. The sole is cleaned out of the dry, dead sole, and the frog is shaped for healthy performance and growth.

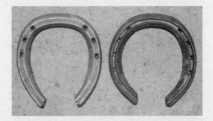

Toe-grip type shoes, or any shoe with increased traction, are not usually my choice. There is a fine line between too little and too much traction. I consider any traction that extends below the shoe's surface to be excessive. We are striving for traction; however, we must also have a certain amount of "give" so as not to put extra torque on our horse's legs. I equate too much traction on a horse to football players playing on artificial turf. When their feet "plant" too much, something must give, and usually it's their ankles or knees. This is comparable to what I have seen in my career with barrel horses. Toe grabs can also be dangerous if your horse overreaches. A toe

The shoe on the left is the one removed from the front foot, while the shoe on the right is the one I shaped for this horse. Notice the bottom portion of the shoe (heel area) is much fuller on mine. I like full, round feet on my horses, very similar to when they are barefoot.

Our new, larger, properly shaped shoe applied to our now level, balanced foot. I am obviously biased here, but it certainly looks better than with the big square toe and contracted heels of the old shoe. Also notice how the heel area of the frog is shaped, allowing dirt to clean out the back. Very nice!

Notice how well balanced this foot is. The shoe is large enough under this horse to sufficiently support his leg and allow good growth through the six weeks between shoeings. The shoe overhangs on the inside because this horse's hoof had been growing to the outside; this practice balances the foot. Also notice how I have rasped off the nail clinches smoothly. This allows a clean pull in case the horse stumbles and does actually pull a shoe. We want the shoe to come off without resistance and stress to the foot and leg.

grab on the hind feet can "catch" the front foot and cause damage from the sharp, extended edge. I have not seen a horse that needed this type of traction, especially when considering my goals of keeping my horses as sound and pain-free as possible.

Bottom line? Use rim shoes and concentrate on finding a farrier who is both competent and willing to explain and listen regarding your horse. Remember, the average time I spend shoeing the average performance horse is two hours minimum to finish all four feet. Any less usually means shortcuts happened.

Level and Balance the Hoof
and Shoe to the Horse's Leg

Take a look at barefoot horses that have been turned out. Their feet are big and round, and their hooves are wider at the bottom than at the top. Why can't farriers maintain this natural shape? Because shoes are too small and contract their feet. We have all had shoes at one time that were too small, and you must

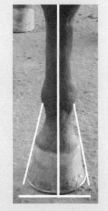

For a horse's foot to evenly strike the ground, the hoof must be leveled using the leg (cannon bone) as a reference. An unleveled foot will cause uneven wear on all areas above the foot.

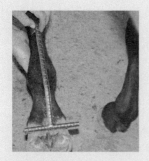

A T-square-type gauge takes the guesswork out of properly leveling the hoof by bringing precision to this most important aspect of shoeing. The hoof side walls must expand at the bottom in order for the foot to properly support the leg. A barefoot horse has the proper growth and expansion; shoeing a horse with a too-small shoe can cause contraction throughout the foot. Blood flow into and out of the foot is very important in maintaining soundness, making it more important to keep the hoof capsule growing large.

remember how irritating that was, right? This process combined with slick, metal shoes instead of rim shoes for traction leads us to the next step: unsoundness.

Most shoers/farriers do not want to place a bigger shoe on your horse in fear your horse will pull it off and they may have to come back and put it on again. The first signs of this practice are a hoof that grows over the shoe before the next shoeing and the collapse of heels. And guess what? Horse owners continue to pull shoes! The feet must be balanced in order to help eliminate this.

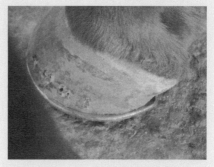

This photo shows how the new shoe supports the side walls and the heel area. Yes, it is a full shoe and may be susceptible to interference from the hind feet while working. However, I have proven that when the feet are balanced, interference is actually reduced.

Questions and Answers

QUESTION I may have a shoeing problem on my 4 yr. old barrel horse. He's been doing very well—w/ just plain steel shoes—no rims or anything! I've used the same shoer for 3 years! However—I don't think he's very experienced at shoeing barrel horses. The biggest problem is a little lacking in drive behind! He's turning very well—but lacks some stride! I've found since

The finished foot, complete with surfboard wax applied to the hoof walls to fill in all nail holes and any open area in the hoof. This method seals the foot from contamination, helping to keep healthy growth.

I began putting shoes on this spring—his stride has decreased even more! Since then—I've asked my shoer if he could drop him down behind—we got him at about 55 all the way around now (which is at a natural angle for him)!—but, my shoer keeps experimenting w/ the shoes—he's set the hind shoes way back so the toe hangs over—he claims this will help him break over sooner!??? Do you want a barrel horse to break over sooner—when you're trying to get a longer stride out of him?

The problem comes in where—I had him re-shod on a Friday—showed him on Sat.—he began rearing before going in the gate (VERY UNLIKE him!). That was 3 weeks ago—& he still seems like something's not right! I've found him to be sore through his middle back—all the way through his right hip! I've had my farrier back out—he doesn't think it's the shoes. My gut feeling still tells me there's something wrong w/ these shoes! Do you have any comments on this setting the shoes back?

ANSWER My first impression after reading your letter is that your horse's problems go beyond the farrier. Equine back soreness is normally secondary to leg problems (except when we are talking ill-fitting saddles, "hot" saddle pads, etc.). I would ask a well-qualified equine vet for a complete soundness exam of your horse's legs with emphasis on his hocks and front feet. The symptoms that you have described are textbook to these types of problems.

Depending on how far back your farrier is setting the shoes on your horse this normally is not a problem. The squaring of the toe is beneficial if applied properly.

Toe- or heel-grip shoes, or any shoe with increased traction, are not my choice. There is a line between too little and too much traction. I consider any traction that extends below the shoe's surface to be excessive. Toe grabs can also be dangerous regarding overreaching by your horse. A toe grab on the hind feet can reach up and "catch" the front foot causing damage from the sharp, extended edge. I have not seen a horse that needed this type of traction, especially when considering my goal of keeping my horses as sound and pain free as possible.

QUESTION Have you ever heard of leaving the toe hanging over the shoe of the hind feet to provide better traction? Would this inhibit a horse from sliding his rear up under him? Would the shoe act as a fulcrum in this position on the foot?

ANSWER Leaving the toe over the front of the shoe causes the foot to break over quicker. Set the shoe back too far and bruising of the sole will result. I have never had this type of shoeing affect my horse's ability to slide his rear up under himself further. Increase in traction? No, this does not increase traction.

QUESTION I have a horse shoer who has been to farrier school, and he was told to take the heel off and leave the toe on barrel horses. He was told that it was hard for a woman to run in high heels, and so was a horse. I have been told all my life that you take the toe and leave the heel. That your horse needs to be on a 55 degree angle if possible, to build the heels. What is right?

ANSWER How about this group of horse shoers we are seeing today? Where do they come up with these stupid sayings and then have the ignorance to live by them? Fifty-two to fifty-five degrees is good for the front feet of our horses. Approximately the same for behind is also in the range we want. I do not get nervous until I see a horse under 50 degrees or over 55 degrees. You are correct in your thoughts regarding preserving the

heels and shortening the toes in general. My horses range from
$3\frac{3}{8}$" in front to $3\frac{1}{2}$" in back in toe length after being properly
trimmed prior to shoes being applied.

It is so important that you have a performance horse shoer
work with you and your horses. Most horse shoers do not understand what is needed to keep a performance horse working and
healthy. Just take a look at the small sizes of horseshoes they put
on horses today. And using flat, plate horseshoes on performance
horse's feet, rather than rim shoes for traction—it is a crime!

QUESTION I feel I have a great farrier. With all the talk recently
about shoes, I have a question. I run most of my horses without
shoes. There is one horse I run with shoes only because she had
been previously run with shoes. I was thinking of running her
next year without shoes. I was wondering if the shoes would
make that much of a difference in performance. My farrier feels
if they don't need shoes, it's better to keep them barefoot. Not
to mention cheaper. I haven't had a problem with anyone going
lame or having hock problems.

ANSWER I suggest you assess the type of ground that you are
running on. Is all the ground that you warm up and compete
on sandy, loam type soil? If so, terrific. If you are encountering
rocks and hard ground, then it is difficult for your horse to stay
healthy with this type of concussion and wear without shoes.
How often you compete is also a concern. If you are going every
other weekend and working your horse on good, deep ground at
home, then you may get away with not having shoes on them.

Like most everything else that has to do with a performance
horse, common sense and logical thought will reveal an answer.

If your horse does well without shoes, then let him go without. The problems that I see throughout the world teaching
clinics are there are so many bad shoers. The hurry-up-and-get-
it-done philosophy is crippling more horses. I wish we could get

away with not shoeing, it is a more healthy way to go. With the amount of traveling that we do and the different (poor) ground surfaces that we compete on, it is impossible to go barefoot.

Keep an eye on your horse's feet and watch for lameness and/or soreness in his soles. Too much wear can cause the sole of the foot to get thin making it sore without shoes, so extra care must be taken. I use a sole paint solution that I put on my horses' feet after each shoeing and in extremely wet climates. This promotes a tougher, harder sole.

QUESTION I read the previous advice you gave on shoeing a horse. I just had my new horse's feet shod for the first time. She is a 4 yr. old and never been shod. The farrier said her feet were good and put just plain shoes on the front and left her barefoot on the back. She is small. 14'1". He said her shoe size was 000. I read where you never put small shoes on, but what about the little feet? Please help me to better evaluate this situation. What would you do?

ANSWER Size 000 shoes on any Quarter Horse is a shame. This is just too small. If for some weird reason this horse had that small of feet (I would perhaps put that small of a shoe on a pony), she would not be suitable for performance eventing. Simply, that is too small of a shoe.

The problem is not you so much as it is the shoers of our world. It is unheard of to shoe a Thoroughbred in this manner, but in the Quarter Horse industry it happens all the time. I suggest finding another shoer who is properly trained and will shoe a horse's feet to the hoof and not to the shoe. Meaning: one that fits a shoe to a horse's hoof without rasping off the hoof wall to make the shoe fit. If they do the job properly the shoe should extend out approximately $\frac{1}{8}$" to $\frac{1}{4}$" from the bottom of the hoof from the first nail hole at the toe area all the way around to the heel allowing room for growth.

You want St. Croix (pronounced "Croy") Lite Rim shoes on all four feet.

Here is a formula and routine to follow:

Front feet must match in:

Size (Size 1 both feet)

Shape (Both feet having same shoe shape)

Angle (using an angle gauge)

A 52 to 54 degree angle in both front feet, and it must be exact in both feet. NO COMPROMISING!

Toe length (must use a measuring tape from the ground to the hairline at front center of the hoof up to the coronet band)

Toe length in front should be approx. $3\frac{3}{8}$" with both front feet having the exact same length.

Must be level (using a level gauge)

Back feet must match in:

Size (Size 2 both feet)*

Shape (Both feet having same shoe shape)**

Angle (using a angle gauge)

A 50 to 52 degree angle in both hind feet, and it must be exact in both feet. NO COMPROMISING!

Toe length (must use a measuring tape from the ground to hairline at front center of the hoof)

Toe length in front should be approx. $3\frac{1}{2}$" with both back feet having the exact same length.

Must be level (using a level gauge)

---

* The extra size shoe behind (size 2) is so the heels of the shoe can be extended. This has been proven by a group of the leading veterinarians in the world, spearheaded by Dr. Marvin Beeman, as attributing to up to a 20 percent longer life of the hock joint by supporting the back of the foot. Think of snow skis with the back portion cut off behind your boots. It would be difficult to feel secure.

** When shaping the hind shoes do not allow the shoer to flatten out the sides of the shoes very much. For some reason the industry thinks this is correct; however, if you show them x-rays of the front coffin bone and the rear coffin bone, they cannot tell the difference so why don't they make the hind feet round just like the front?

The frog should be properly cleaned up of all dead matter and shaped just like in the books. The sole should have all dead hoof removed down to the firm matter. The heel supports growing in from the heels toward the tips of the frogs should be trimmed down. This is for a barefoot horse to have heel support in the wild; however, we are providing a steel shoe for support and, if left untouched, this growth will begin to dry up, die and cause heel contraction.

When shoes are nailed on, there should be enough shoe sticking out from the hoof wall to roll a nickel from the first nail hole all the way back to the end of shoe at the heel area. The horse must never grow over his shoes at the end of the six-week cycle.

I use #5 city head slim blade nails, but most shoers cannot handle this thin of a nail. If yours will, then he is good. If he wants to use the "normal" thick, heavy nail, let it be. Anything that goes wrong they will blame on the nails. Pick your battles and win the big ones. When finished nailing on the shoes and clinching, make certain all nail clinches are rasped thin so if your horse pulls a shoe it will not tear off any hoof wall. No, this will not cause the shoe to fall off! I have proven it for over fifteen years of shoeing the best in the world.

When all finished rasping the clinches, use surfboard wax to fill all of the holes and around all the nails. Smear it over the hoof and rub it down into the holes to seal out moisture and contamination.

This all takes time (approximately two hours to properly shoe all four feet). The job should be beautiful when completed with all four feet looking round, big, and healthy.

•　•　•

RIM SHOES are the minimum necessity on barrel racing horses. They do not have enough traction to cause an increase in hock problems, but quite the contrary. A slick shoe that causes increased slippage does not support the foot's needs for any traction, especially while a horse tries to turn at speed. Place a steel, flat plate to the bottom of your boots and then try and run across slick ground. How do your knees and hips feel now?

Extending the heels of the rear shoes does not cause a reiner effect unless you use a wide, flat plate–type shoe. And come to think of it, why do reiners use a flat shoe? SO THE HORSE WILL SLIDE FOR DAYS! Not something you want your barrel horses to do. It is the slick plate shoe that causes the slippage, not the extended heel (or trailers).

Dental Care

Staying on top of your horse's dental care is extremely important. Periodic exams, maintenance, and corrective procedures are vital. Routine dental care affects the way a horse chews, eats, and utilizes feed. It also plays a role in his ability to carry a bit with comfort.

Oral exams should be an essential part of a biannual exam. Every dental exam provides the opportunity to perform routine preventative care; the end result is a healthier and happy horse. Depending on the condition of your horse's teeth, more than one visit annually may be required to get his mouth in prime working order. By taking proper care of your horse's mouth, he will be more comfortable during performance, utilize his feed properly, and live longer. This all starts when a horse is one year old and every year after.

The horse's mouth is an intricate system that was designed for grazing. The teeth have been perfectly adapted for this purpose. When turned out on pasture, horses will browse almost continuously. The dirt, grit, rocks, and silicate in grass wears teeth. Stabled horses frequently don't give their teeth this workout because feedings are scheduled, not continuous, and they often include processed grains and hay. Softer feeds require less chewing, which contributes to long teeth and uneven wear patterns.

The forward teeth, called incisors, shear off forage. The cheek teeth, which include molars and premolars, are wide and flat for grinding and have a graveled surface for mashing the forage before it is swallowed.

Just like the human, a horse has two sets of teeth—temporary and permanent. The first baby, or temporary, teeth can erupt before a foal is born, while the last of them appear by about eight months. The incisors and the first three cheek teeth start getting replaced at about two and one-half years of age, and by five, most horses have their complete permanent set.

An adult, male equine has forty permanent teeth, while, interestingly enough, an adult mare has between thirty-six and forty. A mare is less likely to have canine, or bridle, teeth. The canine teeth are usually present in mature geldings and stallions and less often in mares. During a normal dental procedure, these canine or bridle teeth are filed smooth to prevent bit interference and reduce the possibility of injury to both the horse and human.

It's important for every horse owner to be able to recognize a potential dental problem. When these problems are present, a horse may show obvious signs like pain and irritation when eating or being ridden. However, they may show no signs at all.

Often a horse will adapt to discomfort. Therefore, it is very important to have periodic dental exams done including a procedure called "floating." Floating corrects abnormalities, removes sharp edges and points, and also helps maintain an even bite. Sedatives, local anesthetics, and analgesics are used to relax the horse and keep him comfortable during floating, as well as during other dental procedures. Having your horse's teeth floated on a regular basis is essential in our champion horse's overall performance and health. This starts at age two, before you even start to work under saddle.

Some telltale signs that your horse may have a dental issue that needs to be addressed are dribbles of feed from his mouth while he is eating; difficulty chewing; excessive salivation; loss of body condition; large and undigested food particles in manure; head tossing or tilting; bit chewing; tongue lolling; bit fighting; resistance to bridling; poor performance; lugging on or grabbing the bit; poor stops and turns; sudden attitude problems like bucking, rearing, or running off; a foul odor from the mouth and nostrils; traces of blood in his saliva; nasal discharge; swelling of the face, jaw, or mouth tissues. These are only some of the signs, and, as you know, each horse is an individual. Remember he may have become used to the pain or discomfort, so being able to detect even the slightest of signs is very important.

It is paramount that you catch dental problems early. Waiting too long may increase the difficulty of remedying certain conditions or may even eliminate correction.

Some of the most common dental problems we experience with horses are sharp points that form on the cheek teeth. These sharp points and hooks can cause lacerations to the cheeks and tongue, even in normal grazing conditions. Because the lower jaw is narrower than the upper jaw, the horse grinds feed with a sideways motion, which facilitates the formation of these sharp points on the edges. The points form on the cheek side of the upper teeth and the tongue side of the lower teeth. An equine dentist will rasp these points down to prevent them from cutting the cheeks and tongue. Some people say that they use a hackamore so they do not have to worry about their horse's teeth. Not true! Pressure from the outside from a tie down or hackamore pushes the cheek up against the teeth, causing sores on the inside of the cheek.

Another common problem is retained caps: temporary teeth that are not properly shed. Extraction of them is often warranted to prevent infections and allow proper development of the permanent teeth. This happens mainly in two- and three-year-olds. Of course that's the time that we want to influence this young horse's world in a positive way.

It is relatively common for horses to loose or break teeth, too. If your dentist or vet finds a loose tooth, he or she will probably extract it to reduce the likelihood of infection and other problems. We have all noticed rocks, sticks, and foreign matter in some hays. The unavoidable presence of such things can often cause chipped, cracked, broken, or lost teeth. Normally, contact with the opposing tooth keeps biting surfaces equal. When a horse loses a tooth, they may not fit together well. When they are out of alignment in these cases, sharp edges are formed. Waves are often formed when a horse has excessively worn his teeth in places or has some teeth that are very long. Most of these scenarios are due to problems like uneven bite planes or misalignment/poor, apposition which can be caused by injury or congenital defects.

If left unchecked, hooks can become long and penetrate the hard or soft palate. While small hooks can be removed with a rasp, longer hooks are usually removed with molar cutters or a dental chisel.

If you experience bit problems, it could be caused by the bit bumping the wolf teeth or long and sharp canine or bridle teeth that are interfering with placing or removing the bit in the mouth.

Wolf teeth are very small and located in front of the second pre-molar. They do not have long roots set into the jawbone like the other teeth. It is rare to find them in the lower jaw, but I have had several mares that did. A horse can have one to four of them or not have any at all. Because wolf teeth cause problems, it is recommended that they be removed at age two to prevent problems, pain, and interference with the bit.

Gum disease and infections of teeth and/or gum material are quite common. These conditions may require antibiotics, extraction, and other specialized care.

The age of a horse affects the degree of attention and frequency of your dental care. Horses going into training for the first time at two to three years old should receive a comprehensive checkup. Their teeth should be floated, and all sharp points and wolf teeth should be removed. They should be checked for retained caps; any that have not been shed naturally should be removed prior to any training to help to make those first experiences positive.

Even yearlings can have sharp points that can damage cheek and tongue tissue. Floating may improve feed utilization, which is so important at this age.

Horses two to five years old may require more frequent exams than an older horse. Because temporary teeth tend to be softer than the per-manent teeth, sharp points can develop quicker. There is also a high degree of dental maturation occurring during this time. Twenty-four teeth will be shed and replaced between two and five years. A horse in this age group has the potential to have between twelve and sixteen teeth erupting at any one time. Horses in this age group should be examined every three months. Remember that even the best care may not alleviate all of your horse's teething discomfort.

Mature horses should get a thorough dental exam at least once a year, or even every six months, even if there are no signs of a problem. It is very important to maintain an even bite at this stage in order to ensure an even surface into a horse's twenties. If you wait too long, alignment might be impossible.

An older horse in his twenties must have teeth examined at least once a year. Because horses can quickly deteriorate when they are older, we need to stay attuned to what is happening in the mouth. Pay attention to body condition and the ability to chew and utilize feed.

Sometimes serious dental conditions can develop, like infections in both teeth and gums; if you see discharge from one nostril, this can signal a tooth problem. These conditions may require surgical treatment or extraction by a specialist.

It is up to us as horsemen to be aware of our champion horse in its entirety. If you notice behavioral or performance problems, dental problems should be considered as a potential cause. Any abnormalities should be corrected, and the teeth should be examined and floated on a regular basis. By including proper dental care in your program, it, too, will be a champion one.

Clipping

Just like grooming, clipping is an opportunity to improve the appearance of your horse while teaching him to behave properly. It teaches patience and discipline. It is the perfect opportunity to be in touch with your horse while teaching him respect and manners. It can also make a wonderful change to his overall appearance. The wild and wooly billy goat look can quickly become the beautiful, refined gentleman look.

Although all that hair serves a purpose in protecting our champion horse from insects and the elements, we can clean up any edges or long, straggly hairs for a huge improvement in his overall look. This will give his head a neater, sleeker, and more refined appearance, his ears and throatlatch will appear more sculpted and trim, and his legs will be cooler and cleaner inside our leg protection.

To clip your horse you will need a set of electric clippers. These are the easiest and fastest tool to use, and they do the best job. Cordless clippers are available that sure make it easier. Make sure your blades are sharp, well oiled, and clean. Make sure all the areas you are going to clip are well groomed and free of most dirt and debris. Although you don't have to wash your horse first, rinsing is recommended. Because dirt dulls the blades, clipping dirty hair is not recommended.

It is also helpful to clip when the hair is damp. This keeps your clippers from getting hot and allows the blades to slide through the hair easier. If areas dry before you get to them, give them a light mist from a spray bottle.

Clip your horse in a well-lit area. If your horse has never been clipped, proceed slowly and be patient. Avoid a situation where he can back up and get away from you. Find another person to help you.

Most horses can be trained to willingly accept this process, but some violently resist. Naturally the buzzing makes any animal suspicious. If you introduce the clippers quietly and slowly and the experience ends without the horse being hurt or being allowed to escape the clippers, you are on your way to a clip savvy horse.

Snap twitch.

Start by letting him feel the vibration at his shoulder and neck and do his legs first.

I would recommend that you turn your clippers on and apply them to your wrist bone. As you will see the vibration against the bone is extremely irritating, so don't ever let the clippers come in direct contact with bone. Believe me, doing it once to yourself is enough to make you be cautious when you're clipping your horse.

If your horse is still resisting, there are several methods of twitching that you can use to help you get the job done. Always apply twitches to the upper lip only.

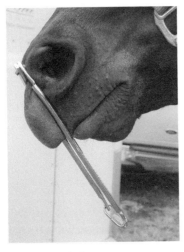

Humane twitch.

At this point you either have a willing horse or one properly twitched. Basic trimming is preferred. We don't need to show clip barrel horses. Start with the front legs; proceed to the hind legs, and then move on to the head and ears. Start at the knee or hock and clip in a downward motion in the direction of the hair,

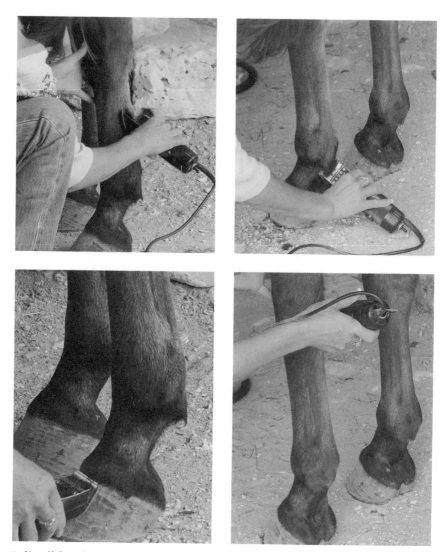

I clip all four legs the same way year-round.

gliding the blades over the surface of the hair with gentle, even pressure, clipping only the hair that sticks up into the blades. Clip down to the ankle or pastern joint. Then finish by starting at the bottom near the back of the hoof bulb and clipping up to meet the passes made when clipping downward. Preferably, remove just the long, straggly hairs. This will keep mud and dirt from sticking. If you are medicating the leg, the product can get to the skin quickly and effectively.

Trim only the outer edges of the ears, leaving all the inside hair. The internal hair is the best defense against mites, ticks, and bugs.

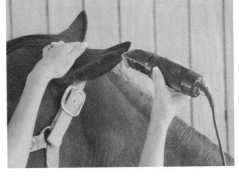

Use your clippers in the "brushing position" to blend clipped areas into unclipped areas. The brushing position is a technique in which the clippers are turned upside down and the edge of the blade is brushed along the tips of the hairs.

After you have clipped the legs, move to the head. Hair and whiskers serve a purpose. The horse uses whiskers as feelers while grazing. They also rely heavily on them in the dark. I don't recommend clipping the hair or whiskers inside the nostrils as they help to filter dust out of the air the horse breathes. Likewise, I don't recommend clipping off the whiskers around the eyes completely, because they help keep dirt and dust out of the eyes. Just clipping the tips is fine.

Start by trimming the hair from the sides and underside of the lower jaw. Work in the direction of the hair growth, using the clippers in a "brushing position." This will remove only the long hairs.

Turn the blades around into the "clipping position" and clip along the bottom edge between the jawbones. Clip upward against the hair growth.

These are the only areas I generally clip, but as you will see, they make a huge contribution to the neat appearance of the champion horse. When you are finished clipping, brush away loose hairs on the horse and, ideally, rinse him. We have all had a haircut and know how uncomfortable those sharp, little hairs are when they start poking us.

Grooming

We are down to the final aspect of taking care of our champion horse. We have properly fed, dewormed, vaccinated, shod, maintained the mouth, and clipped our champion equine athlete. The last piece of the puzzle in his regular care is grooming. If you have been diligent about

Our stallion, Fols Classy Snazzy. I keep all my barrel horses looking as good as possible.

the other aspects of your horse's program, you will find grooming is much simpler, less expensive, and less time-consuming as a result. For instance, with a complete and adequate nutritional program in place, you will find his coat, mane, tail, eyes, ears, nostrils, and hooves are taking very good care of themselves.

The coat will be shiny, sleek, and well moisturized because of the internal production of healthy tissues and natural oils. The mane and tail, as well as the overall hair coat, will grow well and not tangle because it's healthy. The cuticle will naturally lay flat.

The eyes, nostrils, and ears will have an internal boost from nutrients and oils to aid in the production of natural lubricants that act as natural defenses, flushing debris and insects away. The horse's natural secretions will be working efficiently to keep his skin, eyes, ears, and nostrils well lubricated.

The natural oils in the skin and coat create a natural waterproofing. When this horse is rained on, snowed on, sweats, or is hosed off, you will notice that the water will bead up. This helps you get this horse clean and helps him deal with the elements and cool himself through sweating properly. (The healthy horse sweats mostly water, while an unhealthy horse's sweat will contain a high concentration of salts and minerals that dry and dull the coat.)

In turn this beading action assists in quicker drying, because the coat is waterproofed. This is very helpful for many reasons, but especially when cooling out a horse after a workout or competition.

Furthermore, a well-lubricated coat resists mud and manure accumulation. If mud does accumulate on the coat, it can easily be removed. Lubricated hair and hooves compare to a skillet that has been sprayed with a nonstick product. Just as food slides off and does not stick to the pan, natural oils resist dirt, mud, grim, salts, and debris. See how this is already making grooming easier?

The outside of this horse is a reflection of what is happening inside. If he has a beautiful, shiny, well-lubricated exterior, we can assume that is also the case inside his body and throughout his vital organs.

Just like the coat, mane, and tail, the hooves will also show health and vitality because of proper nutritional and shoeing programs. They will be strong, flexible, and grow in a natural way. The sole and frog will also be pliable, yet not easily penetrated by foreign objects. The sole will flex when it needs to dissipate energy during concussion, and the frog will be pliable, yet healthy and strong. In turn it will do its job of pumping blood back up the legs each time it comes in contact with the ground. Hooves are less likely to chip or crack, even if a shoe is pulled. The hairline at the coronet band will not exhibit any signs of drying or flaking. If properly shod, when we run this horse, the hooves will naturally clean out with each step.

The overall appearance of our champion horse will also indicate he is as disease- and parasite-free as possible. Adequate internal lubrication in the digestive tract means parasites will have a harder time sticking and burrowing, minimizing damage. Remember, the outside of our horse is a mirror of what is happening internally. Feeding increases lubrication, which in turn increases parasite control. Parasite control improves hair coat, and so on. It is all connected, like a puzzle.

This is not to say you won't need to groom your horse, but grooming will become fast and simple. Grooming is a way to stay in touch with our horse. We can monitor new blemishes, injuries, scrapes, cuts, swelling, or anything out of the ordinary when we groom our horse.

Instead of working up a sweat trying to untangle a tail or remove mud balls, we can enjoy this time. And as you can imagine, your horse will feel good as well.

Out in the wild, horses aren't groomed. Their bodies clean themselves when they have adequate feed, water, and exercise and are not eating in a confined area where parasites lurk. Owners must take responsibility and do everything we can to help domestic horses function as nature intended.

When my horse looks good, I feel good. A well-kept horse reflects a good horseman with a sound care program.

Groom your horse from top to bottom before and after every ride, each and every time. Start by brushing the coat with a soft- to medium-bristled brush. I like to keep two of these brushes on hand, one that I use after my horse is dry following rinsing or washing and one for when I can't rinse and he is not as clean. This will help keep the coat as clean as possible.

Brush your horse with vigor. Don't be lazy. Vigorous brushing stimulates blood flow and circulation in the skin, muscles, and nerves. In my opinion, vigorous brushing is not intended to clean the horse as much as it is to enhance circulation and blood flow, which also build that healthy coat.

Some horses with exceptionally thick, long manes and tails require a different brush. But in most circumstances, the brush we use on the body works well on the mane and tail, too. Be sure to remove loose body hair before brushing the mane and tail. If your brush isn't stiff and coarse, you can also use it on the face.

You will also need a hoof pick. You should not need to work at heavy picking. If you do, evaluate the way your farrier is caring for this horse's feet. Each time you are with your horse, check the feet. If you remove a rock, stick, or other foreign object lodged in the foot, you prevent further problems, such as an abscess because a rock or other foreign material has been absorbed into the hoof tissues. Once the horse goes lame, a full-blown abscess results as the object works its way out of the hoof. This could have been avoided if you had noticed the rock or object and removed it during regular grooming.

After a workout or competition, find a way to rinse the minimal amounts of salts and minerals that have accumulated on his coat. Again, this will prevent drying of the skin and hair coat.

Of course if it is 25 degrees out, rinsing is not recommended. Walk the horse out until he is dry and then brush him with a brush with soft to medium bristles. You should be able to brush or comb sweated salts off once he is dry with relative ease.

Equine baths are not often necessary. If your horse requires it, don't do it often. When you bathe him, never apply detergent directly to the horse's coat.

First, rinse the horse thoroughly. This is the most important part of washing; take your time. Run water over the entire horse, under his belly, between his legs, and use low pressure when rinsing the head. Rinse off as much dirt and dander as possible. Have a bucket that is filled with a mixture of warm water and a small amount of soap standing by.

Although there are many specialized equine soaps on the market, cheap and simple Joy dishwashing soap has a very low pH and is gentle on our champion's skin, as are baby shampoos and baby body washes, which are all inexpensive and effective.

Suds should be minimal—just a little soap is right. Pour this mixture over the horse and work it into the coat with a sponge, rubber mitt, curry comb, or brush. Then rinse the horse thoroughly. Leave no soap on his skin or coat.

Although conditioning is not necessary, if you like, mix some conditioner with warm water and pour it over the horse. White vinegar mixed in warm water works well too. The vinegar restores the pH balance of the skin after washing, won't dry the coat, and will remove any flaking. If you use conditioner and water, rinse the horse lightly. If you use vinegar and water, there is no need to rinse.

Do condition the mane and tail to minimize breakage. You can also rinse the tail with a combination of a silicone product and water, again combined in a bucket. No rinsing is necessary. Be very careful not to allow any silicone mixture to get on your horse's back, ribs, and girth area. Many a saddle has slid out of position during competition because of silicone.

By keeping your horse well groomed and clean, you minimize the need to wash blankets, cinches, and saddle pads. However, do clean your blankets, pads, and cinches once a year, at the very least.

With only a bucket, a couple of brushes, a rubber mitt, a hoof pick, and a few economical products, your horse will look like a champion. Grooming will become rewarding for both horse and rider, and both will feel good and be comfortable. You will know your horse well because of quality grooming time.

PART FOUR

Champion Tools

What one is in little things, he is also in great.

—Unknown

CHAPTER 7

Champion Tack and Equipment

Train it until you trust it, and trust it before you try it.

—JOSEPH PARENT

Saddles

IT IS vital that your saddle and saddle pad fit and function correctly. Your saddle's main purpose is to fit your horse's back without interfering with movement. It must fit along your horse's back evenly. Minimum cinch pressure should keep it in place. If a saddle fits your horse properly, when you finish working, his back will be uniformly wet. If there is a dry spot larger than three inches, the saddle is putting too much pressure on this spot, compressing the sweat glands. In time this area will become a sore spot, and white hair will become apparent. Once damaged, the dry spot and white hair will be permanent.

Next, your saddle must fit you. Many of the horsemen that I see today ride with a seat that's too large. If the distance between the swells and the cantle is excessive, you will shift around on your horse's back, hindering your horse from working to his maximum ability and throwing him off balance. A horse can run and turn much more successfully without you on his/her back, so make this experience as easy as possible by sitting balanced. Also, if your seat is too big, your stirrups will not hang properly underneath you, which will cause your toes to point down or your feet to shift too far forward.

My trailer's tack room is my home away from home. You can never have too much equipment with you.

When sitting comfortably in my saddle, with my feet in the stirrups and the stirrups adjusted properly, I should have one-half to one-inch between the front of my thigh and the saddle swells. If you are 5'10" or taller, I recommend one inch between your leg and the swell.

Saddle Trees

Regarding the confusing issue of saddle trees—three-quarter Quarter Horse bars, full Quarter Horse bars, etc.—I believe the western saddle industry as a whole does not understand saddle fit. Just look around at any competition, and you will see saddles that are so narrow in the front that they are obviously pinching the horse in the withers (typically the three-quarter Quarter Horse bars). You may notice saddles that sit down in the front and stick up in the back (full Quarter Horse bars), or saddles that appear to fit front and back fairly well, but roll and slide back as the horse moves (full Quarter Horse bars). Saddle tree makers seem to believe that to make a saddle fit, widening or narrowing the width of the gullet to shift the position of the bars on the horse's back is enough. Wrong. The industry basically uses a standard flat bar that they adjust by widening the gullet in hopes of attaining fit. However, the "twist of the bars," or how the bars contour to the horse's back, is the most important aspect of proper saddle fit.

I recommend that you buy a saddle that is endorsed by a competing barrel racer with solid credentials and a proper riding style. Normally, an endorsed saddle has been used and tested on many different horses under varying conditions. Beware of combination trail and sport

☆ Marlene's Saddle Solution ☆

T HE Marlene's Special Effx Saddle has taken the negatives and the positives of present saddle designs into consideration and this has resulted in a saddle that conforms to your horse's back and continues to conform and move as the horse moves and performs. The saddle is not treeless. The top portion of the tree is rigid, like the original Marlene tree, so when you sit in this saddle you cannot tell the difference

Marlene's Special Effx Saddle.

from a traditional all-wood tree saddle. This tree also keeps your body from directly contacting your horse's back, unlike a bareback pad or treeless saddle, which may cause trauma or soreness to your horse's back. We use the original bar twist in the Special Effx Saddle as in my original saddles (designed together with the great saddle maker Howard Council), except the bars are flexible, allowing them to move with your horse. We have seen dramatic improvement in horses that switched over to this saddle.

saddles for barrel racing; they are not properly designed for our speed and turns. Also beware of the "gimmick" syndrome that has become prevalent in the barrel racing world. If a product makes too many claims and does not function properly and logically, chances are it is another gimmick (no matter how many others are in line to try it!).

★ The special Effx Pad ★

W E DEVELOPED a fancy name for my saddle pads, The Special Effx 100% Wool Saddle Pad and the Special Effx II Pad. The end result is a saddle pad that lasts for years and protects your horse's back.

Here are some points that I honestly feel make this pad superior to the others. The Special Effx 100% Wool Pad is available in three-quarter or one-inch thickness. Many "wool pads," are a blend of 60 percent wool and 40 percent synthetic fibers. The best way to tell the difference will be the price, believe me; we have researched this thoroughly. The Special Effx II features a chamois against your horse's back, then topped with one-half inch 100 percent wool felt, finished with a breathable, leather-like material that comes in a variety of colors.

Marlene's Special Effx Saddle Pad.

The pad adheres better to your horse's back and is easy to keep clean. I prefer this pad on horses with low withers. My pads are preformed to fit your horse's back the moment it is put on. We cut and contour the pad adding wear leathers for a durable product that works.

I do not like multiple thin pads and/or blankets—they tend to move around too much. The thick pads with fleece underneath are too spongy and normally made of synthetic materials, which cause heat to build up, and are slick. To maintain my Special Effx pads, I use a rubber curry comb to lightly remove any hair, and then once a year I wash them with Woolite soap, thoroughly rinse them, and then hang them to dry (usually two to four days).

Saddle Pads

A saddle pad must absorb shock and sweat and distribute the weight of your saddle evenly. I always use a three-quarter to one-inch thick, 100 percent wool pad (Marlene's Special Effx Saddle Pad) under my saddles, and I check saddle fit with this pad in place. I do not wear rubber or neoprene, so I do not make my horse wear it either. A dense, breathable, all-natural material works best. There are many saddle pads on the market today that make claims that are simply not true. Remember, a good pair of socks cannot make an ill-fitting pair of boots fit properly. Beware of the gimmicks.

Cinches

Look for cinches that allow the horse to expand his ribs and lungs to full capacity. I use two different styles. My favorite is a 100 percent mohair diamond-shaped cinch with flat stainless steel dees. The second one is chamois-lined EVA (a breathable, non-allergenic material) attached to a 3-inch-wide nylon strap which is attached to stainless steel flat dees with elastic, to allow for expansion of the lungs. This cinch places the no-slip chamois against the horse and is easy to clean. This will aid in maximized run and oxygenation of the blood. Both of these cinches do this.

Mohair string cinch.

Marlene's Special Effx cinch.

Breast Collars

A breast collar's purpose is to keep your saddle from rolling completely underneath your horse in the event your cinches or other strapping

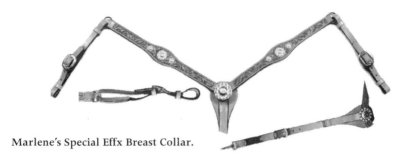

Marlene's Special Effx Breast Collar.

fail. The breast collar should not be used for holding a saddle into position, as this hinders your horse's ability to extend the shoulders to maximum extension. Always attach the strap that runs between the horse's front legs to the front dee of your front cinch. This is also true for your tie-down strap, if you use one. Never attach to the back dee of the cinch, as it will cause your cinch to roll and possibly tear and/or pinch your horse's skin. The tugs that attach the collar to your saddle should be adjusted so they don't restrict the free movement of your horse's shoulders. My tugs are made with elastic to prevent this while allowing them to fit closely to my horse's shoulders.

If you loosen your breast collar and it drops down below the point of the shoulders, take a leather strap, attach it to the breast collar dee, run it over the top of your horse's neck, and attach it to the other side of the collar to hold it in place.

Martingales

There are several different martingale designs available. The only version that I really like and use is the German martingale. This design has reins with loops running up each side for attaching the straps that run from between the horse's front legs. These straps run through

German martingales are my favorite training aid.

the middle ring on my bits—the reins attach to the bottom rings—and then snap onto the reins with easy adjustment for head position. This allows me to pick the headset I want by adjusting the straps to the reins. I don't have to worry about it while working and competing on my horses. This training aid does not restrict the head position or inhibit his run. I have found this design allows the best headset in inexperienced or finished horses.

Tie Downs

Leather nose bands are used when a horse likes to push up against one. You have heard the saying, "My horse likes to balance off his tie down."

Rope nose bands can be covered with rubber, braided nylon, or leather. They are used for competition to keep a horse from resisting the pressure of the bit by pushing his nose out first before he bends it back toward his chest.

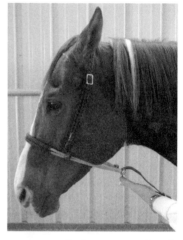

Rawhide, chain, or steel are very severe and are used to teach a horse to not rut out, or fling his head, when you ask for something. I use these for schooling at home, using the rope tie down to run in as long as the horse is doing what I ask during the run.

Rope-nose tie down covered with nylon has moderate severity.

Over-the-poll tie downs are for a horse that carries his head high but keeps his nose tucked or for a u-necked horse. They help such horses balance and use their hind ends effectively. When adjusting these, make sure the piece that goes in the front hangs down just above the eye. It can be made of rope, steel, or chain depending on how severe you need it to be. Be careful when you first put this on; I suggest you

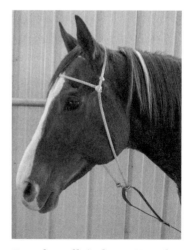

Over-the-poll tie down. Note the position over the eyes.

Single-ear leather headstalls are my favorite.

move the horse around in a pen while you are on the ground, to get him used to it.

Headstalls

I prefer an all-leather headstall; they adjust easily no matter how old they are. I like single or double sliding ear pieces that will allow adjustment to match where your horse's ears set on his head. Headstalls with brow bands have limited adjustment and can interfere with the eyes of your horse. Comfort and flexibility are my goals when choosing equipment.

Overreach Boots

These boots protect the front feet in case the back feet overstep during a run, potentially bruising or cutting the bulbs of the feet. They must contour down the back to fit properly and have a double hook and loop fastener. I also use rubber pull-on overreach boots. They are hard to put on and take off but work very well, especially in mud.

Overreach boots.

Polo Wraps

These leg wraps are made of polar fleece, with very little stretch. They are thicker than any other type of wrapping bandages. I use these in competition. When training at home, I use my new boot designed with cool and breathable materials that are lightweight, with perfect fit. They allow for flexion of the ankle and offer even support when applied properly. They are manufactured by Ortho Equine Products and available through World Champion Designs catalogs.

Polo wraps.

Cavesson

A noseband should be used whenever you use a dee ring or ring snaffle bit. These bits do not have curb chains; a horse may open his mouth when pressure is applied. The cavesson will discourage an open mouth and provide more control. I prefer leather types that are round at the front and flat on the sides, with unlimited adjustment.

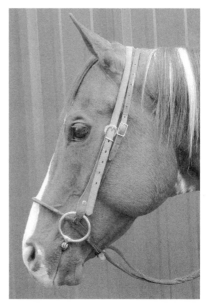

Cavesson.

Spurs

I use spurs with rowels every day that I ride my horse. When competing, I

Sidewinder spur.

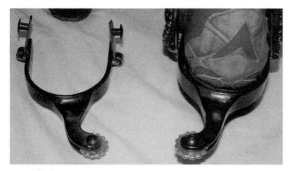

Roweled spur.

take them off as long as my horse is listening to my leg cues. If he is not, I first try the sidewinder spur, which may be just enough to accomplish what I need. If not, I use my roweled spur.

Bits

Dee-Ring
Snaffle with
a twisted
mouthpiece.

Marlene
three-piece
gag.

Long-shanked
snaffle.

Hackamore.

Ported bit.

Wonder Bit.

Dee Ring Snaffle with a twisted mouth piece is my favorite bit to use when working on flexion and bend.

Marlene three-piece is my favorite bit to use when competing. It has one inch of gag motion and a two-inch shank.

Long-shanked snaffles are good for competition or putting whoa on a horse. If you choose to use this to compete, realize that your horse may get stiff. But if you use the dee ring bit three days a week, you should be fine.

Hackamores are okay for competition if the horse needs more run or has an injured tongue. They will get a horse stiff and again the dee ring bit used will keep this from happening.

Ported bits are very effective for whoa and rate. Do not be afraid to use them to enforce good control. I use this bit on the day I choose to sprint my horse.

Wonder Bits have a three-inch diameter gag motion; I feel this is too much for most of my horses. It is a very slow reacting bit, and I find a horse learns to get away with things when using this bit.

You will see that when you find bits that feel good to you that you will use the same bit on most of your horses. It takes four or five bits in your collection. By using different bits on your horse each week you will eliminate horses that get picky about different bits. When fitting all bits, I put them so they touch the corners of the horse's mouth and create one wrinkle. If you do not do this, the bits will have slow reaction time. You can find all this equipment and more on my Web site at www .WorldChampionDesigns.com, or call 1-800-542-8225.

Bit guards are used on all gag bits to prevent the bit from pinching the sides of the horse's mouth. Choose thin ones with a small center hole. This type is made for western bits.

Bit guards.

Reins

I prefer leather reins that are braided with five pieces of leather to create grip and width. Leather will break if my horse steps on them. I put a brass snap on at least one end of the reins so when I get off my horse the first thing I do is unsnap the rein so I can hold on to them better.

Tack is an investment that I will have for the rest of my life. Buying equipment tested by professionals that have credentials in the performance horse world will help you, but common sense still is your best judge.

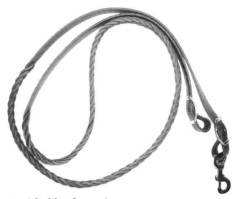

Braided leather reins.

Questions and Answers

QUESTION I noticed in one of your answers to someone that you said you like to keep a horse out of a tie down. Could you please explain why you do or do not like a tie down?

ANSWER Thank you for your question regarding the use of tie downs. The unique aspect of barrel racing as a sport is the fact that we are working with animals that are individuals. Generalizations made in our industry such as, "I do not like tie downs. . ." are incorrect. A tie down or any other piece of equipment that is necessary to enhance a horse's performance is an obvious good idea. With this said I would prefer a horse to run and work without a tie down only because I feel this gives a horse the ability to balance on his own and may increase his speed by allowing him to reach more with his nose while running. This is why we do not see racehorses with tie downs on. However, the horse that I won the world championship on, Dutch Watch, ran in a tie down, along with many of the other great horses in our industry. Once again it takes logical thought and unemotional analysis to determine what works best in each unique situation. This is also why I feel my clinics have been as successful over the years, as it is difficult to analyze problems in search of solutions without the proper experience.

QUESTION This tie down thing has really got me confused. Some people tell me my horse needs a tie down, and some tell me she does not. She won't listen to me when we are running down to the end pole (Pole Bending) or whenever. When she is taken out in a field or pasture and walked, she is great. I'm just tired of her head slinging up whenever she is under pressure. Roping and Poles are the worst. My mom wants me to keep working with her slow so hopefully she will be ready to haul some this summer. I think she is very capable of doing what we want, if we can get this habit solved. If you would have any solution at all, please e-mail me back and I would appreciate it greatly.

ANSWER You are right in realizing that your horse's head slinging is not acceptable. I suggest a stronger noseband such as rope wrapped with a smooth wire or a rawhide nose piece. Adjust the tie down strap so when the horse is standing in a normal position, you cannot touch his throatlatch with the

I am demonstrating the adjustment for a snug tie down. I cannot touch the throatlatch of this horse when he is standing in a comfortable position.

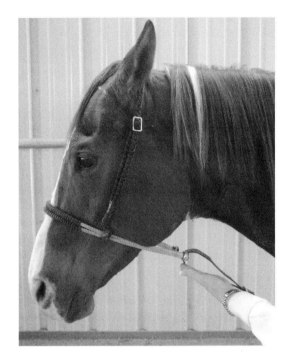

strap. Do not get it too tight or you will restrict her ability to flex and bend. You want it to apply pressure only when she has her head in the wrong position. Many times when changing head equipment I place it on my horse, adjust it, and allow the horse to stand in her stall, or put her in the round pen to get used to it on her own. Start out with it on the loose side and then snug it up according to her attitude. You will not be able to fix this problem in one day, so give her three or four days of this before proceeding to an alternative.

One alternative is to put a steel noseband on her and adjust just as described above. A few hours a day with this headgear on while being turned loose to get used to it will surely help her attitude and head position. Use this until she learns to stop the head slinging then go back to a less severe noseband, leaving the tie down length the same.

QUESTION I'm currently training a barrel horse. He runs well without a tie down. I started him with a running martingale, to keep his head set. Do you feel a tie down gives the horse more balance even though he is running at ease without?

ANSWER If it is not broke, do not fix it! A tie down is not necessary and, as a matter of fact, can be a hindrance to a horse that is not used to one. Watch a horse race and count all of the tie downs being used.

I use a tie down on a horse that either needs some assistance in maintaining his nose and poll position or when I have a horse that likes to "brace" against one. Many horses are able to gather and set better when they have a tie down to "push" against.

QUESTION I have a really nice four-year-old Stricken Six mare. She came off the track with an 89 speed index. I bought her last November, trained her, and started hauling her to jackpots this summer. My question is: Her head pops up in the turn on the second and third barrel which loses a lot of time. My husband says she needs to be faster in her turns. What is a good way to keep a horse's head down plus making her faster in her turns? I currently use a tie down on her. Thank you for any help you could give me.

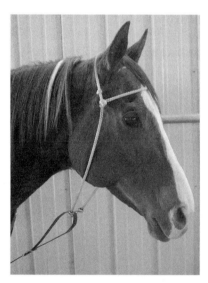

Over-the-poll tie downs need to have the tie-down strap very snug to work well.

ANSWER Thank you for your question. There is a new style tie down on the market that works well in solving the problem that you are experiencing. This tie down fits behind the horse's ears and has a nose piece. This tie down system holds the horse's poll position more level. I have tried a few different manufacturers of this style of tie down, and many come apart in a short time. I suggest you contact World Champion Designs at 1-800-542-8225 and get their Rope Poll Tie Down, as it is the best I have used.

QUESTION My question is what is a brain chain? Is it the same as a chain eyebrow tie down?

ANSWER A brain chain runs over the over the poll and has a chain that runs over the top of the eyes. It is a severe treatment for a horse that is exceptionally high headed and/or wants to rear up and elevate in the front end. Be careful when using something as severe as this as it can cause the horse to intensify his behavior. You can get it in a rope type—I prefer it to the steel or chain. I have seen good results with this type of head-gear. I like that it does not restrict their nose position to ensure I am not restricting their ability to run to maximum ability.

QUESTION What a great Web site for us new barrel racers! I would like to thank you for your time dedicated to this!

My question is on how to determine the length of rein when you are barrel racing. I have tried different lengths and types of reins, and am not sure if too long has an effect on his neck reining ability, by this I mean he reacts to the direct rein and then when it touches his neck, he reacts to that by getting out of position. Any help would be greatly appreciated!

I recently bought your Special Effx saddle and love it! Very comfortable and great on the horse!! Thanks again for you time.

ANSWER Through my clinics and watching others at competitions I have found most have their reins much too long. They may be comfortable at a walk and slower paces, but once we begin to run the pattern, too long reins are detrimental. It is so important to be consistent on our horses, and having your reins too long makes this extremely difficult, since placing our hands in the same position down the rein at each barrel becomes more difficult. It will also cause you to get your rein

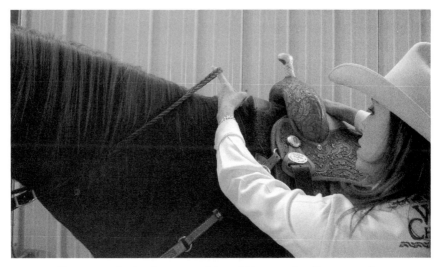

Proper adjustment of reins for competition riding or schooling around the barrels.

hand out over the barrel in a turn. This will get you out of balance on your horse's back.

I like to use the rule of thumb of applying pressure to my reins, while sitting in the saddle, and having four inches in front of my saddle horn to the reins as they become tight. I also like to place tape down each side equally where my hands need to be when approaching a barrel. Consistency is the answer your horse is looking for.

CHAPTER 8

Champion Travel

Well-arranged time is the surest mark of a well-arranged mind.

—Sir Isaac Pitman

WHETHER you are hauling your horse down the road a mile to a friend's or across the U.S. to a rodeo, the truck you drive, the trailer you tow, and the way you care for your champion horse are important pieces of the champion puzzle.

The safety of you, other drivers, and your champion horse takes some diligence.

Tow Vehicles

Whether you have a beautiful one-ton dually, a Ford Explorer, or a classic pickup, the recurring themes are safety, function, and maintenance. Your vehicle must be large enough to handle the trailer and load you're towing. Although a half-ton truck or recreational-type vehicle can handle a small two-horse trailer, it isn't up to the challenge of a three-horse trailer with living quarters. Read your manual to understand the recommended towing capacity of your vehicle. Then compare that capacity with your trailer to make sure you are within those limits. The weight listed by your trailer manufacturer is the unloaded weight of your trailer. Take that number and add in appropriately for your horses, tack, feed, and the various equipment you'll carry to arrive at the estimated gross trailer weight (GTW). That's the load your vehicle must haul—safely.

If you have a truck with single rear wheels and you're towing a trailer with living quarters or one that's heavy, consider having an adjustable air springs system installed on your truck. These are relatively inexpensive and can be adjusted with an air compressor to level your load and improve steering and braking.

Make sure you have a functioning trailer brake control installed in your vehicle. When adjusted correctly, this device allows your vehicle and trailer to brake together. This is the source of more problems than any other aspect of towing safety. The wire harness must be spliced in at least two places during installation. Over time, those wires are vulnerable to dirt and vibration. One electrical short and you lose your trailer brakes. Then you have a trailer loaded with live, moving weight pushing you through that stoplight or down that steep grade.

Make sure your tow vehicle has large, easily adjusted mirrors on both sides. You have got to see what is going on behind you. Be aware of blind spots.

Make sure your hitches are installed properly by a reputable company. Request heavy-duty reinforcement. In accidents with gooseneck trailers this could be the only thing that keeps your trailer from turning over if someone broadsides it. Always attach the emergency braking cable and safety chains. Check your battery and cables to the emergency braking system once a year, or every six months if you use your trailer often.

Keep your hitch ball greased. Each time you hook up, make sure there's enough grease there to prevent grinding while you're driving. Dry wear will weaken the coupling of your trailer, opening the door for your trailer coupling to break or crack and possibly break free.

Maintaining Your Tow Vehicle

Whether you do it yourself or take it to the shop, stay on top of vehicle maintenance. Not only will this increase the useful life of your vehicle, but it will increase chances that you and your champion horse stay out of the breakdown lane. Breakdowns happen, and we will talk about that, but minimize the possibility with maintenance.

Because of the years of experience that I have putting lots of loaded miles on various tow vehicles, I can tell you there are three things that will make your tow vehicle last: clean air, clean fuel, and clean oil.

Change your fuel, air, and oil filters as often as the manufacturer recommends. These three simple things increase your tow vehicle's life.

Be diligent about your brakes. Although trailers have brake systems, never rely on them solely. Making sure your tow vehicle is able to stop quickly can save you. Check the trailer brake control as well before you leave home. Depending on the weight you are towing, adjust your controller to manufacturer's specifications for the weight you plan to haul. Don't forget to adjust it after picking up two of your friends and their horses.

Always make sure your tires are in good condition, with the proper amount of tread and air pressure. Air pressure is one of the most overlooked details—use a tire gauge and be sure all tires have equal pressure. Proper air pressure will prevent blowouts and contribute to quick braking, better handling, and increased fuel mileage. Be diligent about this. Check your tire pressure before you leave home and look at the tires each time you stop for fuel or gas.

You would be amazed at how tire pressure will fluctuate between the time you leave home and each of your stops. This is due to the heat that is generated when we are moving for any length of time. Air temperature also greatly affects tire pressure. If the outside temperature is 100 degrees, you know that asphalt is going to be even hotter. If it is -15 degrees, the asphalt and your tires will be cold.

Remember those science lessons? When air is cold, molecules move slowly and take up less room; air pressure decreases. When air is hot, molecules move fast and take up more room; air pressure increases. See how these principles apply to tire pressure and why they impact it?

If tires don't have enough air, the weight of the vehicle and trailer will push them flatter, so more surface area contacts the road. That means your vehicle will have to expend more energy to get down the road, reducing gas mileage. It will be harder to stop your truck and trailer by delaying braking and creating uneven wear on your tires. As you know, this not only wears them out faster, but puts them at risk for blowouts and flats.

Proper tire pressure also makes your vehicle handle better. If you notice your vehicle pulling to one side, not braking properly, or being hard to manage, pull over and check your tire pressure. Try and rotate your tires every 5,000 miles. You will be amazed at how much longer tires will last just by keeping them properly inflated and rotating them frequently.

Regularly check all your other tow vehicle fluids as well: transmission fluid, brake fluid, wiper fluid, coolant or antifreeze, and so on. I recommend you learn how to do these things yourself. Learn from your shop mechanic or a friend. Take an active role to increase confidence. You will feel more comfortable with your vehicle on the road.

Trailers

Regardless of the type or size trailer you tow, safety, maintenance, and function apply.

Let's start with safety. Make sure you hook up to your tow vehicle safely. Attach safety chains and the emergency braking cable, plug in the electric cable, and check the lights.

Once you're loaded, double-check that your coupling is locked and the pin is firmly in place. You can't be too careful. When I am thinking of these things, I am not worried about my trailer coming off my ball while driving smoothly down the road, which of course is unlikely. It's the other driver who is not paying attention I worry about.

Maintain your trailer. Grease bearings, check brakes, and maintain your tires, check tire pressure, and rotate your tires often. This will alleviate uneven wear problems, which we frequently see on trailers.

Some of the newer trailers don't require that you repack wheel bearings, but you need to maintain them with gear oil. This is simple. Be active—learn how to do these things.

Depending on your trailer's braking system, you may need to check hydraulic fluid. Be sure there is an adequate amount of it to facilitate proper braking when you need it.

Every few months, get under your trailer. Make sure there are no wires or hydraulic hoses hanging. Check for cracks or anything that needs to be addressed.

Maintaining Trailer Interiors

Let's move inside the trailer. As far as maintaining the inside of your trailer, the most important thing is the floor. Depending on the type of trailer, you will either have an aluminum, steel, or wood floor.

Urine is public enemy number one to our trailers. It is very acidic, and large amounts can irritate the equine respiratory tract. It pits aluminum, rusts steel, and rots wood. It is paramount to keep the inside of your trailer clean.

After every trip, take a few minutes and clean the interior out. Periodically pull your mats and clean under them. I prefer three-quarter inch thick mats. Although they add weight and are harder to pull and manage, they do provide better absorption of concussion. If your floor is wood, sweep it. If it is aluminum or steel, hose it out and make sure you let it dry completely. Also make sure you wash your mats, both sides.

When your trailer is dry, sprinkle baking soda on the floor and then replace your clean, dry mats. The baking soda will balance the acidity of the urine when it comes in contact with the floor. This practice definitely makes aluminum floors last longer and neutralizes future ammonia.

Once you have replaced the mats, I recommend that you place a couple strips of duct tape over the cracks between them. I don't worry about drainage because I am diligent about cleaning my bedding and interior; urine will be absorbed by shavings and then removed. I recommend tape because shavings work their way under the mats on long hauls from vibration. Not only does this ruin the edges of your mats and stretch them out, but it is a tripping hazard during loading and unloading. After taping the mats, sprinkle more baking soda on top of them and then add fresh bedding.

I recommend shavings for bedding. About a two-inch depth is perfect. As you drive down the road, vibration will shift bedding toward the back of the trailer. Redistribute it often for this reason.

Avoid bedding that's too deep, because it is not comfortable for the horse if shavings ball up under the heel in an awkward way, stressing tendons during travel. Too shallow and we defeat the purpose of them altogether. Ideally shavings are there for absorption. Your mats are for comfort. Ultimately your horse's hooves should be in contact with the rubber, with a small amount of shavings inside the foot. This puts some pressure on the frog to help stimulate blood flow. This can be a great help to our horses. With a small amount of clean bedding in the foot, the up and down motion of traveling will stimulate the frog and pump blood up the leg.

Also, some horses will not urinate in the trailer at all unless there are shavings to avoid being splashed. We don't want these horses holding urine, so use shavings, especially for long hauls.

To reduce flies, I fill a pump-style sprayer with a fly spray mixture. Before you load your horses, pump it up and give the interior and bedding a quick misting. Mist walls, dividers, and especially the ceiling to keep your horse comfortable in the summer.

If your trailer has rubber matting up the sides of the walls, spray the sides with Armor-All after you have put your bedding in. Make sure it does not get on the floor matting; it can be slick. This will keep manure from sticking to the wall matting—dried manure on walls is like cement and very hard to remove.

Next, check your roof vents to make sure they are functioning. Check your latches, dividers, and springs. As you may know, aluminum, while light and easy to clean, is softer and does wear quickly. Make sure all latches and hooks are in good condition.

Trailer Function

Go for a ride in your trailer while someone else drives. You will gain a whole new perspective on what is going on back there, trust me. This definitely will make you more conscious of your horse's comfort and also make you a better driver for your horse.

The most important aspect of trailer function is interior size. Please make sure your horse has enough room to travel comfortably. If all you can afford is a two-horse bumper pull trailer, by all means purchase a Thoroughbred-type trailer or an extra-wide one. Your horse must have enough room to be as comfortable as possible.

There are two different styles of trailer loading, ramp or step-up. Either is just fine. However, be sure your horse will load in either style trailer. You never know when you might have to switch your horse to someone else's in an emergency. We don't want to be fighting with a horse to load on a ramp for the first time along the side of the road.

Mangers create storage galore and a neat little feeding area, but they are a hindrance to your horse during travel. Not only do they cut into his space by a foot or two, but they do not allow the horse to put his head down, which is essential for proper esophagus function and sinus drainage.

Besides colic, "choke" is the next most common travel-related health problem seen in horses forced to eat without the ability to lower their head. The feed creates a blockage and often enters the airway as the horse struggles to breathe. This opens the door for infection and life-threatening pneumonia.

Another problem I have experienced with mangers is that a big horse cannot turn around and get his head past the divider anchor next to him to get out. Although we want our horses to back out, you may come across a horse or someone else's horse you are hauling that just won't back out. This is a major problem and dangerous to both the horse and the handler. Horses can hurt themselves and do damage to you and your trailer.

Instead of mangers, I recommend feed bags, not nets. As you know, nets are dangerous because horses get bored and play with or tug on them. We don't want to risk a horse getting a foot caught. Trust me, your horse doesn't have to be wild or unruly for injuries to happen.

Make sure the feed bags are at wither or chest height if possible. This of course depends on trailer design. Don't tie your horse in the trailer, so he can eat and lower his head periodically. If your horse has room, feeding hay on the floor is also okay, especially if you let horses eat while you eat or rest. It is difficult for a horse to eat off the floor when the trailer is moving, however. It is also dangerous since shifting can cause him to hit his head or lose his balance. So, when *you* stop and eat or take a break, let them eat off the floor. Between feedings, clean out hay bags or remove them all together to avoid hay particles blowing around and into his eyes during travel.

I really hate to see trailers going down the road with horses' heads hanging out. Although it looks cute to the family-filled cars going by, it is a terrible practice. Make sure you have window bars or screens in place at all times. Horses can easily lose an eye from road debris. All it takes is a vehicle or semi to go by, throw up a rock, and then your champion is blind in one eye.

Horses have also been killed by bolts and other objects flying into an open window. At the rate of speed we are traveling, such debris can completely pierce the skull of a horse and kill him. Insects are also a problem. Bees hitting and stinging horses is common with open window travel. There you are driving along, singing to the radio, while your horse has been stung in his muzzle, his airways closed from the swelling. You'd never even know something was wrong until it was too late.

Because screens rot and tear from the sun and wind and you cannot get to your horse's head with them on, bars are a better option. The hardware from screens can break and wear out from constant air pressure. When you get to your barrel race, you want your horse well rested. That won't be true if a screen was flapping in his face for five hours straight.

Let's discuss road vibration and concussion. If you can afford it, consider air-ride suspension on your trailer. This is money very well spent. It makes an enormous difference in your horse's comfort. A horse can handle a very long period in the trailer, but not constant motion, vibration, and bouncing. Because he can't move, leg circulation is limited. Keep this in mind if you are traveling with a friend and have limited time to get somewhere. If you have rodeo-ed heavily, you know what I am talking about. You may be switching drivers and hauling hard. Make sure you stop and get your horses out. Move them around. Give them the chance to get blood pumping down to their legs. If you are in a situation where you can't find a safe place to get your horse out, at least stop the trailer for a time and let his legs rest.

However, with extra effort you can always find a place to safely unload and get your horse out. Make this a priority. Ideally you need to do this every four to five hours.

Consider placing an outdoor thermometer inside your trailer in a location where you can easily see and read it when your horse is inside, perhaps against the wall between the horse area and tack area. If you place it on an outside wall, you may not get an accurate reading, especially in cold weather. During cold weather, you can tell when to add or remove blankets. In hot weather, it will help you determine if you should water or unload the horse more often.

Ceiling insulation is also a very good idea in both hot climates and cold. It can be done at the factory or after market. There is a product that can be sprayed directly on the ceiling which dries in place and is very effective. Although not pretty, it does serve its purpose very well and is inexpensive.

It is a great idea to install of couple of 12-volt fans inside your trailer, one in the front and one in the rear. Place them out of reach. You don't want horses chewing on them or bumping their heads. Place the back of the fan so that it pulls air from outside in; locate the switch so you can turn them on from the outside of the trailer. This feature adds to your champion horse's comfort.

Loading and Unloading

Your horse needs to be schooled on loading and unloading when young. If you are having problems with an older horse, work at this before you need to go somewhere. Take your time and be patient. The ultimate goal is for the horse to see the trailer as a comfort zone.

Your horse should load willingly and quietly. He should also back out of the trailer. Although you often see people turning horses around and jumping them out, it is best to have your horse slowly and willingly back out with his head level.

If you have a horse that runs out backward, don't pull on his lead. He will resist the pressure and back out even faster, raising his head higher. Let him leave on a loose lead and then know you have some schooling to do after he is out.

Backing a horse out of a trailer is really a necessity. Your horse will have to back out if he has any size to him and he is ever loaded into a trailer with mangers. You might find yourself in a situation where your horse is the last one loaded into a trailer with a permanent tack compartment in back. If your horse won't back out, you are now in a jam and so is your horse, since he can't turn around. You will see "equine panic" like never before.

Teach your horse to load and back out properly before you ever let him get all the way in the trailer. Open the feed door so he can see light and have some type of feed for him to eat after he gets in for reward. Let him put one foot up, then back him out. When he does this slowly and with ease, let him put both front feet up and then back him out. Progress to three legs. He should readily put one hind foot up if you have worked slowly with the front feet. Ultimately, you want to get all four legs just inside, and then have him slowly back out of the trailer, one foot at a time, in a trusting way. This only takes a few sessions and is definitely worth the time spent.

If you need to use grain or treats to tempt him in slowly, do so. Be sure you only reward him with feed after he has made a positive move. Give him a tug, and then release the pressure. Give him the choice to step up. Horses give to pressure, but only if the pressure is released at some point. Do not face or look at the horse you are leading.

If he flies out of the trailer, don't give him a treat. Give him one when he quietly places and holds one foot up in the trailer and one when he gently places it back out. Treats or feed given during this process releases endorphins in your horse's brain and can help make this a good experience. This is the foundation for making the trailer a comfort zone with a horse that resists loading.

Once you get your horse loaded, never tie him into the trailer. If you should have an accident and your trailer overturns, the chances of a neck fracture and death are very likely. This is the number one cause of fatality in horses involved in trailer accidents. A horse that is not tied can also balance himself during travel better. As we already discussed, a free head also plays a role in eating and preventing respiratory problems in the trailer.

Additionally, tying a horse in the trailer is the fastest way to get in a wreck. Horses often panic after you tie and leave them in the trailer. They followed you in, so naturally they want to follow you out. It is at this time they realize they are tied, feel trapped, and pull back. This starts a domino effect. The horse then hits his head on the roof, flies back, often breaking his lead or trailer hook, and of course you are in the middle of this storm as your horse backs right over you or pins you against the wall. This is a bad spot to be in and a quick way to watch the comfort zone of the trailer disappear for both horse and handler.

Until your horse lets you leave him, standing quietly once you have led him in, have someone close the gate behind you. Your horse will be less apt to think about unloading. It is also helpful to open the window, if there is one, and have someone at the horse's head to help keep him in one spot until you get a gate or divider closed. If you have a horse that keeps getting his head over or around the divider, tie him with a piece of baling twine. It will break if the horse hits it hard enough, and in time you will not need to tie this individual anymore.

Comfortably on the Road

I am often asked about leg protection in the trailer. Because of heat created and loss of circulation, I do not like leg wraps during hauling. Keeping blood flowing down and back up the legs during hauling is challenging enough without hindering it with pressure.

The horse paws and kicks because he is losing feeling from lack of circulation or his legs are hot. Next thing you know, the wrap is halfway undone and he is stepping on it. Of course this will always be the horse loaded in the front with three behind him. Then you have to unload and rewrap, just to have it happen again.

The only time I would even consider leg protection in the trailer is if I had a horse that kicked or was hauling with a horse that kicked. Even if I do, there are other ways to handle it besides wraps. I don't want this horse to hurt himself and certainly not the horse next to him. If you have to use protection, choose loose fitting shipping boots. You can also put a bell boot on any of the four feet of both the kicker and the horse next to him to protect coronet bands.

A better fix would be to have your dividers fitted with removable rubber that hangs down to the floor. This will limit airflow for the horse, however. It is nice to have a removable divider in your tack room so if you are hauling another horse that you don't know well or one that kicks, you can protect your champion. This is a safe backup plan.

If you have a horse that travels badly, there are several things you should consider. Pay attention to how you are driving, first of all. You may have helped create this monster. Slow down for turns; wait for your trailer to complete a turn, not just your truck, before accelerating. Brake smoothly and slowly, and try to never weave around. If you ride in a trailer, and I suggest you do, you will be more conscious of these things.

Your horse may be a bad hauler from a traumatic experience. There are several options to make him more comfortable. You can open a divider and let the horse ride loose, which I do whenever possible. Let him travel backwards, which is more comfortable for many horses. Make sure if you do this there is a stall in between horses so he doesn't bother the other horse.

To discourage a horse that kicks, the last thing you might consider is a leg chain. These are very, very effective. A fleece-lined leather

A size 0 shoe fits the ankle of most horses.

strap with a short length of chain attached buckles around the hind ankle. When the horse kicks, the chain reprimands him. This may sound cruel, but a horse wearing it will usually only kick once. This is a much better option than having your expensive trailer torn up, or opening the door to discover bleeding, swollen legs.

If you use them, put them on after the horse is loaded, and take them off before you unload him. You can also use a horseshoe and put it on the pastern area just like you put a bracelet on your wrist. Turn it around so the toe of the shoe is at the back of the foot, and when he kicks, it will hurt enough to encourage most horses to stop.

Before you begin a trip, plan for making stops every four to five hours. Also offer your horse water every four to five hours. It is a good idea to travel with water from home. If you use a plastic tank to bring water from home, make sure you clean it out with a baking soda solution at least once a month. Let it air out and dry completely before recapping to avoid a plastic or sour taste and smell. If your horse is not drinking his water from home, you may have this problem.

If you don't bring water with you, invest in a water filter that attaches to a hose. These are widely available and made specifically for traveling with livestock. They contain charcoal filters that remove impurities and neutralize offensive smells and tastes.

Travel Requirements for Your Horse

No matter how frequently you travel or how far, always keep a copy in your vehicle of your horse's registration and insurance policy if he has one, plus a picture of your horse for identification. You never know when your horse might get loose or wander off, or even be stolen, no matter how diligent you are. Missing horses can happen to the best of us. Ready identification can minimize the severity of the problem.

If you are going out of state, you will need a Coggins/EIA test and a Health Certificate. Coggins tests are valid from six to twelve months, but each state has different requirements as you'll see on the list provided. They were current at the time this book printed; however, requirements change so check them often.

STATE	COGGINS/EIA TEST Period of Validity, in months
Alabama	12
Alaska	6
Arizona	Not required
Arkansas	12
California	6
Colorado	12
Connecticut	12
Delaware	12
Florida	12
Georgia	12
Hawaii	3
Idaho	12
Illinois	12
Indiana	12
Iowa	12
Kansas	12
Kentucky	6
Louisiana	12
Maine	6
Maryland	12
Massachusetts	6
Michigan	within calendar year
Minnesota	12
Mississippi	12
Missouri	6

STATE	COGGINS/EIA TEST Period of Validity, in months
Montana	6
Nebraska	12
Nevada	6
New Hampshire	6
New Jersey	12
New Mexico	12
New York	12
North Carolina	12
North Dakota	12
Ohio	6
Oklahoma	6
Oregon	6
Pennsylvania	12
Rhode Island	12
South Carolina	12
South Dakota	12
Tennessee	6
Texas	12
Utah	12
Vermont	12
Virginia	12
Washington	6
West Virginia	12
Wisconsin	within calendar year

As always call before you haul! Be sure and check with each state that you will be traveling through for the latest requirements. Your veterinarian can help you with this.

A health certificate is good for 30 days, and all states require them. The states that also require brand inspections are Arizona, Idaho, Nebraska, Nevada, New Mexico, Oregon, Utah, Washington, Wyoming, Colorado, and Montana.

Lay-ups

When you arrive at your destination or rest stop, your first priority should be to let this horse rest and lie down. It doesn't matter if it is 3 AM and you have been driving all night. Your horse must be your priority if you want him to perform well and stay healthy.

Over my entire career, I have never tied a horse to my trailer overnight. There is always somewhere to put this horse. It may take extra effort, but you need to find somewhere for him to rest. Whether it is a calf holding pen, a rodeo arena, or a lay-over facility, that little extra effort is required for a champion.

Check his accommodations carefully for safety. Get a flashlight and take a good look before you unload. I have driven on to another place when I found conditions unacceptable for my champion horse. Remember, safety comes first. Check for wire, nails, sharp objects, loose boards, or broken latches. Be sure it is clean and manure-free.

Your horse is going to want to roll. Make sure the area is big enough and he can't get a leg trapped under a board. Don't risk letting your horse get hurt. If there is an arena or pen for turn-out, make sure all the gates are closed and that it is safe. Lead him around awhile first to get the blood flowing. Turn the horse loose and let him move around and roll a few times while you prepare his pen. Avoid letting him buck and run hard, though. This could cause an injury.

Hang a couple of his own water buckets securely after you rinse them, then fill them with your water from home or filter the onsite water if possible. He needs to drink and hydrate himself. Avoid setting a bucket on the ground for three reasons. First, he may dump it over. Second, the wire bails on a bucket can hurt our champion horse. Lastly, dirt, shavings, and feed can contaminate the water.

Keep his environment clean. Horses like familiarity, just as we do. Use his own feed pan or bucket, and keep to your routines as much as you can.

If the ground is hard, put down some shavings. Bring some along or shovel some out of the trailer; don't make your horse lie or stand in a hard pen all night. Dust is very irritating to our horse's respiratory tract. If the ground is dusty, or you put out a new bag of shavings, lightly hose them down to rid this area of dust.

Finally, check the latches again. I always tie the gate shut with my lead rope. I prefer an open pen to a stall, which gives my horse more room to move around—he needs it after a long haul. He will also get a lot of fresh air outdoors. If the weather is poor or a stall is the only choice, repeat your safety check. If there is a top door to the stall, secure it open in case it gets windy.

If you're on the road the following day, and you have the chance, ride your horse before you leave, even if for only twenty minutes of walking. If you have more than one horse, pony the other. If you have more than two, take turns. I would sacrifice twenty minutes of sleep to ride before loading up and making my horse face another day in the trailer.

Your horse's comfort and safety always come first; check his surroundings thoroughly, avoid dust, and keep him safe, well cared for, and comfortable.

Emergencies on the Road

There are two types of emergencies you may face while traveling: horse-related or related to you or your vehicle.

Horse Emergencies

Horse problems can range from colic and injury to heatstroke, snake bites, or fractures. As a horse owner, you must know how to respond promptly and take the right action. You need to know how to recognize distress in your horse. That's obvious if your horse is cut or bleeding, but in more subtle cases you need to look for certain signs.

First, you need to know what is normal. The pulse rate should range between thirty to forty-two beats per minute. The respiratory rate should be between twelve to twenty breaths per minute. Rectal temperature normally ranges from 99.5 to 101.5 degrees. If your horse's temp exceeds 102.5, get a vet immediately. Temps over 103 indicate a serious disease or disorder. Capillary refill time—the time it takes for color to return to gum tissue after you press and release it—is two seconds or less. Test skin pliability by pinching or folding a flap of neck skin and releasing. If your horse is dehydrated, it won't immediately bounce back in place. Try this at home so you will know what's normal. You also need to know your horse's normal behavior patterns and watch them closely. All of these tests should be tried at home under normal circumstances.

The mucous membranes of the gums, nostrils, and inner lips should be pink. If they are bright red, pale pink, yellow, white, or bluish, this usually indicates a problem.

The color, consistency, and volume of excretions should be typical of the horse's normal pattern. Straining or an inability to excrete manure could indicate colic.

If your horse seems lethargic, distressed, anxious, and uncomfortable or won't eat, take a closer look. Check for normal gut sounds. If you hear nothing or they are very loud, suspect colic. Listen at home when your horse is well. Listen to him at different times of the day and before and after he eats. Then you will know when there is a difference or problem.

As far as injuries or lameness goes, watch for head-bobbing, reluctance to move, an odd stance, unwillingness to get up from a down position, and any bleeding, swelling, pain, or heat.

Watch for tying up, paralysis, or seizures. These various forms of muscle cramps range from mild to serious and life threatening.

No matter what emergency you face, mental rehearsal of vital steps will better prepare you. Stay calm. When you are done panicking, your problem will still be waiting for you to handle it. Here are some guidelines for preparing for emergencies.

Always have your veterinarian's number on your speed dial, near your phones, and in your truck. Know how to get in touch after hours. Always have a back-up veterinarian in case you can't reach your normal vet. Have an atlas or map ready so when you do get help on the phone, you can establish a direct route to get to a clinic if necessary.

Try to get someone to assist and help you if you are alone. Even a stranger or someone passing by with no horse knowledge can hand you things and lend moral support.

Prepare, store, and keep a vet kit stocked for an emergency. Your traveling vet kit can be elaborate or simple, based on your skill, knowledge, and amount of time you spend on the road. Again, take an active role. Know what's in your kit, what it is used for, and how to use it.

Stay calm, try and keep your horse calm, get your animal to a safe area in case he goes down, get professional help, and find someone for moral support and assistance if you can. Know your horse's vitals before you talk to the vet, relay them clearly and completely, along with the condition of your horse. Listen closely and take notes. Don't administer sedatives or tranquilizers unless you know that the circumstances warrant it or a vet has instructed you to do so.

Again, rehearse these emergencies, know what to do, and be familiar with different treatments. Keep your first-aid kit nearby and a phone line to a vet available. Time is critical. Don't worry about overreacting or bothering the vet. Be quick and calm and you will minimize the consequences and damage.

Human Emergencies

Of course, people can have emergencies out on the road too. Have a first-aid kit ready for yourself. If you are tired or sick, do what is necessary. Don't risk your horse's life or your own by driving when exhausted or sick.

Have extra cash and credit cards available for emergencies. Have a reliable atlas with you. You can get laminated ones at truck stops. Highlight your routes so it is easy to read your travel plan. You can easily wipe off the ink from laminated maps later. These atlases also have city maps of large cities. That helps you get through them with a trailer. You don't want to be lost, driving your horse all over the place trying to turn around. You want to get your horse where he is going as quickly and safely as possible.

Make sure you have a cell phone and that bill is paid. It is never good to be on the road without a phone.

If you get a flat tire or blowout, pull off the road. If the blowout is on the driver's side, try to get off a ramp and park on the left of the road to avoid danger from cars going by. If you must pull off to the right, get as far off as you can. Put on your flashers and put out a reflector at night.

Get the tire changed as quickly as possible, then drive until you can get off safely at an exit. Then pull over and recheck everything, including the lug nuts.

Be smart and be safe about it. I purchase AAA travel insurance; they have helped me more than once. Make sure you get the RV insurance so they will take care of your trailer too. If you don't know how to change a flat, you should not be out there driving your champion around. Learn how. If you can ride a horse, you can change a tire. Learn as much as you can if you plan to be out there on the road. The more problems you are capable of handling, the better. The faster and more efficient you are at handling emergencies related to your truck and trailer, the safer you and your champion horse will be.

CONTENTS OF EQUINE FIRST-AID KIT

Adhesive Wrap: Vet Wrap and Elasticon tape	Triple Antibiotic Ointment
Adhesive Tape (like duct tape)	Hemostats
Antiseptic Solution or Betadine Scrub	Latex Gloves
Acepromazine	Peroxide
Banamine Paste	Pliers
Benadryl or Dexamethasone	Probiotic Paste
Phenylbutazone Paste	Razor Blade
Cotton Roll	Rectal Thermometer with String and Clip
Standing Bandages and Wraps	Sharp Scissors
Cling Wrap	Sulfa Tablets (SMZ)
DMSO Gel	Tongue Depressors for Applications
Easy Boot	Rubbing Alcohol
Electrolyte Paste	Twitch
Eye Ointment	3cc Syringes
Eye Flush	12cc Syringes
Furacin Ointment	20cc Syringes
Gauze Pads—Assorted Sizes	19-gauge $1\frac{1}{2}$-inch needles

CONTENTS OF HUMAN FIRST-AID KIT

Advil	Cold Packs	Saline Eye Wash
Aspirin	Hot Packs	Tape
Tylenol	Matches	Tweezers
Band-Aids	Plastic Bags	Scissors
Benadryl	Rubbing Alcohol	
Blanket	Peroxide	

CONTENTS OF TOOL BOX

Batteries—variety of sizes	Open End Wrenches
Wood Blocks—2'x6"x2"	Overalls
Chains for Cold Weather Travel	Pocket Knife
Duct Tape	Rags
Electrical Pliers	Rain Jacket
Electrical Tape	Roll of Paper Towels
Engine Oil	Rubber Mallet
Extra Electrical Plug	Reflectors
Extra Bolts, Nuts, and Washers	Screwdrivers—various
Flares	Socket Set
Flashlight	Spare Gas/Fuel Container
Fire Extinguisher	Spare Filters
Fuses—various sizes	Spade Shovel
Fuse Pliers	Spare Tires (truck and trailer)
Gear Oil	Speed Wrench or Lug Nut Wrench
Hammer	Tire Pressure Gauge
Hydraulic Fluid	Transmission Fluid
Ice Scraper	Vise Grips
Jack	Wiper Fluid
Jumper Cables	Wire
Light Tester	Wire Cutters
Mud or Snow Boots	Work Gloves
Oil Funnel	

TRAVEL LIST FOR YOUR HORSE

Hay

Grain

Electrolytes (I like the 707 brand)

Water

Bedding

Buckets—two for each horse

Hose

Supplements

Spray Nozzle

Manure Rake

Manure Shovel

Extra Halters and Leads

Spare Horse Shoes

Horse Shoe Nails

Hole Punch

Clinchers

Hammers—shaping and nailing

Snaps

Chicago Screws

Electrical Tape for Wraps

Twitch

Utility Sprayer for
Interior Trailer Spraying

Fly Spray

Fly Sheet

Fly Mask

Light, Medium, and Heavy Blankets

Box Fan and Extension Cord

Tack

PART FIVE

Champion Execution

*We are what we repeatedly do. Excellence, therefore,
is not an act but a habit.*

—ARISTOTLE

CHAPTER 9

Champion Barrel Racing

No matter how far you have gone on the wrong road, turn back.

—TURKISH PROVERB

Conditioning

CONDITIONING and exercise may be the keys to making championship dreams come true. The warm-up, which we do every time we ride before we ask the horse to work sets the scene for success. I believe that a fresh horse cannot focus on his rider or think, so it is our job to ride him the perfect amount of time before we ask him to go to work.

I realize a lot of us work and have family obligations, but ultimately we need to condition six times a week, with one day off. However, if you can only manage three days of conditioning, your program will probably work fine. Because we are trying to produce champion execution, I assume you are under a six-day program.

Four-mile Warm-up

Let's start with the foundation to our conditioning program. All of my horses are ridden or ponied four miles a day prior to any other work. Total time is about twenty-five minutes. I start with walking my horse, then I trot, lope, trot, then walk again. I warm up and condition both sides of the horse, loping on the left lead the same amount of time that I do the right. So, keep track of direction over time and distance.

When I move into the trot or the lope, I want the horse to really move out. We are not training for pleasure here; we are training for high performance. Try to not pull on the reins any more than you need to, and keep your legs relaxed with heels down; sit upright in your saddle. Horses interpret leaning forward in the saddle with our shoulders in front of our hips to mean "let's go fast." This is why: when we ride at the walk, our posture is very upright and a horse feels the weight of our body in the middle of his back. When we want speed, we lean forward and rise up out of our saddle to remove weight from his back. It does not take many rides on a horse until he figures this out, so be aware of you posture at all times when riding your horse.

Help him relax and warm up his muscles up slowly. If your horse is acting lazy and moving without energy, encourage him to move out. If your horse wants to be a speed demon, sit even deeper in your saddle and make sure you have a bit with plenty of control, like a long shanked bit, or ride in a hackamore. Use your voice gently, saying "easy," and steady the horse with your reins. Your goal is to have the horse trot and lope on a loose rein, the first lesson to teach your horse.

Walk a quarter of a mile, then trot three-quarters of a mile. Lope one mile on one lead, then lope one mile in the other direction, without slowing down except to change directions. For the fourth mile, energetically trot for half a mile, then slow trot the second half. This is the entire four-mile warm-up. Each horse is different; if your horse is nervous, I suggest walking one extra mile before or after. Four miles seems to condition a barrel horse perfectly, contributing to your objective to prevent injury to your horse during training or competition.

Breezing or Sprinting

Every third day, sprint, or breeze, your horse after the four-mile warm-up. We need to make sure barrel horses are capable of running their best. Young horses, unless they have been on the racetrack, have to learn how to run with weight on their backs. Begin this the fall of their three-year-old year. Sprint for a quarter of a mile on a straight strip of ground with good footing that has no holes and is safe. Open him up

and let him really exert himself; if he feels like he needs encourage-
ment, ask him by tapping lightly with your legs in a smooth, consistent
rhythm and make a kissing sound with your voice.

A horse has two types of muscle fibers. Those for fast, explosive
efforts are called fast-twitch muscle fibers, and those for steady efforts
of long duration are called slow-twitch muscle fibers. Sprinting/breez-
ing is the only way to condition the fast-twitch fibers on a horse new
to a high speed event like barrel racing. Speed work also builds up
the horse's lung muscles and increases lung capacity, both required in
barrel racing.

If you are making competition runs on this horse during the week,
there's no need for more speed work unless your horse is not running
as fast as you know he can. It is easier on a horse's body to sprint in a
straight line than to run the barrel pattern, so see which one is best for
your horse to accelerate to his maximum run.

Bringing a Horse Back into Condition

Perhaps you have a horse that has been turned out, and it's time to
start riding him again. The first two weeks, ride two of the four miles.
You want to bring his heart rate up, work it, and then bring it back
down. Trot one mile, then lope a half-mile on one lead, then lope the
other half-mile on the other lead. Condition both his sides evenly.
Walk him for as long as it takes to cool him out or get his breathing
back to normal.

After two weeks, increase to three miles for two more weeks. Trot
the first mile, lope the second mile, half a mile on each lead, and trot
the third mile. Again, you are bringing up the heart rate, working it,
and then bringing it slowly back down.

By the fifth week you will be ready for the normal four miles.

During the fifth week your horse is in good enough shape to start
back on the barrels at a lope. In the sixth week, when you finish your
third mile, you can work your horse on the barrels, at a run, or sprint
your horse in a straight line.

After a lay-off, it takes about five or six months to get your horse in
optimum condition by exercising every day and adding competition
runs. If a horse in top shape were to get injured and need to be laid

off work, it takes about three months before he loses complete body condition.

If you choose to pony (lead a horse off another horse) another horse, make sure the horse getting ponied is staying in the proper gait to benefit from a full workout.

After I have finished my four miles, I work my horse on the barrel pattern for ten to fifteen minutes, and then I put him up.

A horse that I am just starting on the barrels will get worked on the pattern for this amount of time, six days a week; I don't want to bore him, so I keep the sessions short. As soon as I feel he knows the pattern, I decrease the work on the barrels to three times a week. How many weeks it takes to teach him the pattern will depend on how well broke he is to start with.

A horse that I am taking to jackpots is worked two to three times a week on the barrels. The farther along a competition horse is in his career, the less I work him.

I work all horses on horsemanship maneuvers at least three times per week. I work on their fundamentals, so that there is no misunderstanding of what I am asking a horse to do. I use several different exercises involving barrels twice a week, to keep them from getting bored with the same old barrel pattern and keep them listening to me. I like to do other jobs with my horses, like working cattle or roping off them. You can teach your horse other speed events, like pole bending, which will increase his value if you are to sell him. These new skills and exercises prevent or fix any problem areas in your barrel runs. I'll discuss these in depth in the following chapters.

WEEKLY PROGRAM A mile at a trot averages about seven minutes, and one mile at a normal lope takes about five minutes. Time your horse, because each one goes at a different speed. Then when you are in a small area or arena, you can time yourself and know just about how far you have ridden.

My six-day schedule always includes the four-mile warm-up. Three days per week I work on horsemanship; one day per week I work on exercises with barrels; one day per week I make a competition run or do other events; one day per week I do pattern work at the walk, trot, and lope. The last day I rest my horse. This is the complete program for conditioning your champion horse.

Horsemanship

You now have your champion program and champion tools in place. So you're sitting there on your conditioned champion horse ready to get to work. What's next?

The first thing we need to establish is if our horse is broke. We lightly touched on this, but let's refresh. The term "broke" means he willingly executes basic horsemanship maneuvers with ease and without resistance or hesitation. If your horse is already broke well, then your job will be to keep him tuned up. I am going to tell you what horsemanship maneuvers you should work on weekly to keep your horse sharp. If your horse is not broke, that's okay too, because I am going to tell you how to get him well educated so you, too, can get your horse broke, work on these horsemanship maneuvers weekly, and keep your horse sharp. In both cases, this process will make a better barrel horse that lasts for many years.

This part is our foundation for execution. If he can execute these basic maneuvers, he can run barrels. In barrel racing, we combine the talents of a racehorse and a reining horse. Even if you never show your horse in reining, it is important to have a horse that is able to do reining maneuvers well.

If you practice them three times per week, your horse will understand what you are asking of him when you school him on the barrel pattern. A horse that understands the basics of horsemanship will not become frustrated. Additionally, you will become a better rider through these maneuvers, which is how you stay sharp as a rider.

A champion rider and a champion horse must be able to execute a few basic maneuvers well. Although they are simple, it does take effort, time, and practice to achieve precision. As a rider, we must be able to get our horse to execute all of these maneuvers at the walk, trot, and lope, with the same precision.

We have to add some pressure, in the way of speed, to both the horse and ourselves at home in our arena. If we don't, when the time comes to put that pressure on, responses won't be reliable. Get your horse used to willingly executing them under speed and pressure. Then when you make an actual run, you and your horse are comfortable and know what to expect. You'll know how to react and how to use these maneuvers to get your horse where he needs to be. Your horse knows how to respond and use his body properly, and both horse and rider can get it done at speed.

Before you begin, remember you have three aids to utilize when asking your horse to do something: your voice, your hands, and your legs. You also have four places on your horse to use them: the head and neck, the shoulders, the rib cage, and the hips. You have got to use all your aids on all these parts of the horse to communicate and make him work for you. If you do not, then a piece of the puzzle will be missing.

The Warm-up

Begin by riding the complete warm-up, described earlier in this chapter. Because a fresh horse cannot think, always warm up before doing anything else. Not only does this condition your horse, but it warms up and relaxes you both and focuses your minds for work.

During the warm-up, don't pick on your horse. Let him relax and warm up his muscles and mind. I use this time to prepare myself mentally and determine what my main focus is going to be with my horse today. This plan will determine what bit you'll be using to execute it. For instance, if your focus is going to be on his stops, you will need a bit that has more shank. If your plan is about getting the shoulders more flexible, the bit you choose will have less shank.

I try to have a plan before I leave the barn, so I can have the proper bit on to start with, unless I have an individual that requires a bit that gives you plenty of control in the warm-up. Never let a horse know he can take control of you at any time, always have the upper hand. When you're done warming up, walk back to your riding area, make a bit change if your game plan requires it, and begin your maneuvers.

Maneuvers

There are only seven things we need to work on during horsemanship. Leads, flexing/bending, counter-arcing, moving off your leg, stopping, rollbacks, and backing up. To accomplish these at speed may take three or four years. Refresh your horse's skills weekly.

Leads and Circles

Let's start with our leads. First you have to know when your horse is in the correct lead. If you are loping in a left-hand circle counter-clockwise), your horse's left front and hind leg should reach ahead of the right legs. To clarify, leading means that the left legs are ahead of the right legs or vice versa. There are several ways to determine this; you can look down, but this is not recommended because it throws your weight forward and off-balances a horse's stride and positioning. The way that I prefer to teach is to just look at your legs. Glance down, with your eyes only, keeping your chin up, and you will note that your toe will be closer to the horse's elbow of whichever leg is leading. If you only use your eyes, you won't change your body position. You can also feel your hip on that side pointing farther forward. Try to learn how to feel the difference without looking. If you can't, just glance down with your eyes only, to look at your toe.

How do you ask him to take the correct lead? Lope a circle about 40 feet in diameter, tip his nose to the outside of the circle, squeeze with your outside leg, kiss to him, and slightly lift out of your saddle, encouraging him to lope. This should cue him to take the proper lead. If he takes the wrong lead, immediately bring him back down to the trot and then repeat your aids and cues. If he takes the wrong lead, be immediate with your response for correction so he understands that he did it wrong. Once he takes the correct lead, change the pressure of the rein to the inside rein and ask him to position his nose toward the inside of the circle. Squeeze with your inside leg slightly and push him toward the outside of the circle, making him shape his body round to match the circle you want to lope.

Remember, circles are round, not square or oblong. To keep them round, apply constant pressure with your inside leg and steady tension on your inside rein. If you want to slow him down, use your outside rein as your brake, making sure you never change the tension or position of your inside rein. Your weight should be in your outside stirrup, so you are balanced for your horse. The outside stirrup weight should not shift your saddle in that direction. Apply pressure with your inside leg to the rib cage to keep him bent and loping the size circle you want. Your hand should always be above the swell of the saddle and in front of your body. This will keep you balanced and

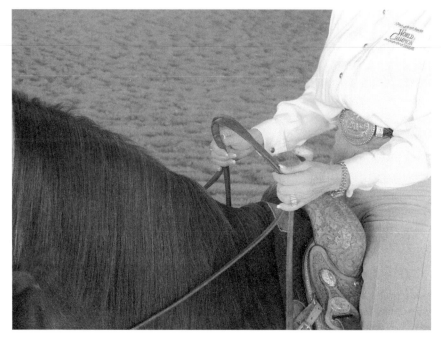

Correct hand position.

prevent you from leaning to the inside of the circle with your shoulders. Your chin and eyes should always be up, aimed in front of your horse's head; never look down at your hands or the side of your horse's head. That would cause you to lean forward and rise out of the saddle, making the horse go faster and reducing your control of the shoulders or hindquarters.

Now ask your horse to lope a smaller circle, about 20 feet in diameter, by closing the outside rein or moving it in closer to his neck. Release some pressure with the inside leg and use your outside leg and voice to keep him going. Don't let him slow down or break into a trot. Think of your outside hand and leg as the speed regulator and the inside leg and hand as the shaper. I am not sure there is such a word, but it does describe the job.

When you ask your horse to lope a smaller circle, sit deeper, encouraging him to use his hindquarters. Sitting deeper is accomplished by exhaling and feeling your spine sink down into yourself. The arch in your back goes out, and your horse will feel you melt into your saddle seat. From the other maneuvers, this horse is going to understand that you sitting deeper means he needs to gather his hindquarters up under himself. When he does this in a smaller circle, he'll bring the inside hind leg up under himself as a pivot leg. It will stay forward as he keeps loping a nice, tight circle. If you need to slow him down, say "easy." If you need to speed him up to keep him loping, squeeze or tap with the outside leg and make a cluck or kissing sound.

After your horse executes the small circle well for three rotations, let him move back out into a large circle by opening up your outside rein, moving your hand out from the neck, and increase inside leg pressure. Work this maneuver in both directions. I do not mind how fast a horse begins the big circle, because a horse will usually slow down to a comfortable speed after realizing that he is only going around this one way. I try not to pick fights because I know the maneuver I am doing is going to correct the secondary problem. Anyway, barrel racing is a speed event, not a pleasure class. The bit I would choose for this ride is the dee ring. Horses should do this well in every bit.

Flexing

Now on to flexing, or bending, your horse properly. Remember that a horse's nose leads him and his body will follow. If walking to the right, his nose should be tipped to the right. The shape of his body will dictate the maneuver he executes. The bit I choose as my bending or flexing bit is the dee ring snaffle. Let's get started softening, suppling, flexing, or bending him—words that all have the same meaning.

I prefer to use split reins when working on horsemanship. Keep them well oiled to prevent them from being slick; this will help with keeping the proper length between the bit and your hands. If your reins are too short, you'll be pulled forward in the saddle and lose control of his hindquarters. If they are too long, you'll have to lean back or lift your hands too high to make contact with the bit. Reaction time is also delayed if your horse makes a wrong move. The reins should be over the saddle horn and swells, your elbows near your sides, and only two to four inches of movement should be needed before you feel the bit come in contact with the horse's mouth.

This is what I see when I am sitting on my horse and asking him to flex or bend his head and neck.

Make sure your reins are the proper length and that you are sitting in the middle of the horse so he's well balanced. Position his head in the direction you want him to go. The outside rein should be open and off his neck, while the inside rein begins to add some pressure; this is called directional reining. At the same time, apply pressure with your inside leg, as discussed for loping circles.

The inside leg pressure rounds, or arcs, his rib cage. The pressure provided with the inside rein arcs his neck and brings his nose closer to my leg. When done correctly, his body is shaped like a half moon, from the tip of his nose to his tail. If you apply too much pressure, he is going to move toward the outside of the circle, losing control of the hindquarters. Releasing the inside pressure brings him back into a balanced state of the shoulder and hip underneath you. Try to see one eye of your horse; if you can see the forehead or both eyes, this is too much bend.

We want barrel horses to respect our legs and be sensitive to them. One of the easiest ways to achieve this is to wear roweled spurs. I wear my spurs during my horsemanship maneuvers to soften my horse's sides and get quick responses. Your horse will only feel them when you turn your toe out from the side of the horse and direct the spurs into his sides. At other times, the inside of your leg and foot ask him to respond. If he doesn't, lightly tap or bump him with your spur between the two cinches. If you are spurring your front or back cinch, then your legs are not hanging directly under you as they should be.

Barrel horses need to be fluid in both directions, but just like humans, they will have a stronger side. It's your responsibility to work harder on the weak side so that both sides feel even.

Start by walking in a circle; add leg pressure and inside rein pressure. Check that you can see his eye and that your hands are above the swells of the saddle in front of you. Feel him moving away from inside pressure toward the open outside rein. Release your leg pressure; you will feel him stop moving away. Remember to keep the pressure with the inside rein quiet and steady and always pay attention to your arm and hand position.

These are the basics of flexing and bending. You will need your horse to execute this maneuver again in both directions and at the walk, trot, and lope with the same precision. Remember to add pressure with speed. Your flexible horse is needed for proper execution of the next exercises, as well as for running barrels properly.

Counter-arc

To counter-arc means that your horse's head and body will be arced the opposite direction of travel. This exercise allows the rider to move a horse's shoulder, a maneuver we do every time we leave the first barrel, or teach a horse to run straight to the next barrel, or home.

Start by traveling in a circle. Pick up your outside rein, tipping his head to the outside of the circle, and apply outside leg pressure to shape his body. Open up your inside rein so this horse has a place to go. If you feel him crossing his front legs, then he is doing a counter-arc. Let him know he did a good job. Remember, horses are claustrophobic; you have to offer a place for them to find relief.

Start in a large area, on a large circle, so your horse doesn't feel bound up. Always take him back to that comfort zone. Once you have completed the counter-arc, remove pressure and let him move back out to the large circle, the comfort zone where he can relax.

Once you can execute this maneuver at the walk in both directions effectively, add some pressure. Do it at the trot. When he masters that, again in both directions, move to the lope.

Flex his head to the outside of the circle and push with your outside leg. Open the inside hand. The inside front leg of your horse should really be reaching out so you can see his shoulder opening up or moving out. Really sit back and encourage him to keep his hind legs up under him, and keep your weight off the shoulders to allow him to move them freely. Keep your chin up and look ahead to keep his shoulders free. As soon as you feel him take two or three steps, let him relax.

This beneficial exercise opens the horse's shoulders, allowing you to move them side to side. This is one of the lateral movements we are going to use often in a barrel pattern.

Side Pass

We have worked the shoulder, neck, and rib cage. Now we need to work on controlling the hip in a side pass maneuver. We will be doing this by moving our leg back a little farther than we have been and applying pressure.

To help him learn to side pass, face him toward a fence to keep him from wanting to step forward. If he wants to back up, put his butt toward the fence. To side pass to the right, tip his head to the left and open your right rein. Applying pressure with your left leg, between the cinches, and ask him to move away from that leg pressure. Using your left spur at this time may be necessary. If he doesn't move smoothly or evenly, move your leg toward his shoulder or hip, whichever is lagging behind. Apply pressure evenly and release it as soon as he moves the correct direction.

Apply the proper hand and leg pressure; your horse should see that the positive move is away from the pressure in the only open direction. As soon as he moves, release the pressure so he knows he did what you wanted. You may only get one step each day, but this is enough. Avoid overbending his head and neck. If you do, you won't be able to control his hindquarters.

The side pass gets horses moving away from leg pressure and allows you to control the hip and shoulder. This is important when keeping a barrel horse parallel to the barrel before starting the turn. The bit I choose would be the longer shanked bits.

Stops

Use a fence as a training aid to help you get your horse to stop reliably from just sitting down deep into the seat of your saddle, saying whoa, and lightly pulling on both reins evenly. This allows your horse to make the choice to stop by feeling or hearing you. This is a great way to start teaching any horse how to stop properly. The less I have to pull on this horse, the better, and it makes me have lighter hands.

At a walk, head squarely toward a fence or a 90-degree corner. Sit deeply about ten feet from the fence; when his head is two feet from the fence, say "whoa" like to mean it, then apply light and even pressure on both reins as you gather them. Use your legs to keep him square up with the fence. He will try to go left or right the first few times. Do all this in steps, so he stops with his head right up against the fence.

Always maintain your posture when slowing a horse down or stopping. Keep your elbows in close to your body, back straight, legs directly under your hips, and the heels of your boots down.

This picture shows the rider leaning too far back, with the heels of her boots not down, and the reins too long. Avoid this very poor form.

Graduate to a trot, and then stop from the lope and then gallop. Do the exercise until you are doing it well at all three gaits. Don't be afraid to add some pressure and speed to it. Don't get into a big hurry with it, though. We have to progress at the rate the horse does.

Continue until he is really listening to the cues; sitting down, saying whoa, and applying that light, even pressure to the reins. It isn't a jerk or quick move of the reins, it's a gather. Keep your elbows in, thumbs up, and the heels of your boots down. Think of your hands as rubber bands, with some give to them. Don't release and then pull again. If you release him, he will drop onto his forehand and bounce you out of the saddle. For good smooth stops, the weight of horse and rider shifts toward his hindquarters.

The goal of this exercise is that he gathers his hindquarters as soon as you sit deep and comes to a stop nicely when you say "whoa" and apply rein pressure. Allow this horse to stop—don't hurry it or force the issue. I use a bit with a long shank on older horses; if this is a two- or three-year-old, I would have him in the dee ring snaffle.

Backing Up

To encourage your horse to use his hindquarters and round his back muscles, use a lot of reverse, or back up. Because the front end of the horse is heaviest, we have to constantly work to keep elevation and lightness to the front end and shift weight back to the hindquarters.

We start teaching barrel horses to back up when they are babies, on the ground. They should do it in response to voice command and pressure on the halter. When we get on their backs, we have established a good foundation and understanding.

Start the back-up maneuver with about ten inches of rein between your hands, with each hand on either side of his neck in front of the swells of the saddle. This will allow you to control both sides of the horse and keep his head low. Gather him up slowly and back him up smoothly with even pressure on each rein. Tap with the sides of your feet up by his shoulders once he starts moving to give him momentum.

If your horse does not back up, hold one rein tight and give him a little snatch with the other rein. Snatch and release, snatch and release, and keep him straight with your legs when he does start to move. Do this until he takes one or two steps.

If you try to force the horse with a hard, straight pull back, he is more likely to stop and get very stiff all over; that is called sulling up, or spitting the bit. Steady, constant pressure doesn't explain what you want.

Instead, use the word "back" and take and release with one rein and use your legs to help with momentum. You can also have someone on the ground, off to one side, tapping his chest and saying "back," too. If he only takes one or two steps, stop asking and reward him by releasing the pull on the reins and rubbing him on the butt. Try this over a few sessions and I think you will have good results.

Rollbacks

After you are sure all the other maneuvers are being done correctly work on the rollbacks. A rollback is a 180-degree turn. It teaches a horse to pull with his front end and drive or push with his hind end. You will need all the cues that you have taught the horse to accomplish this.

To execute a rollback properly, sit deep, stop, take one step back, tip the nose in the direction you want to go, and then push him with your outside leg to accomplish the 180-degree turn to reverse direction.

Picture yourself walking your horse down the white line on a road. Keep your horse's hind feet on the white line, stop, back up, tip the nose and using your outside leg, walk the front feet off the line and around to face the other direction. He needs to walk around, not hop, keeping his hind feet on the line until facing the other direction.

To get your champion horse doing this smoothly, go step by step. The first thing he needs to do is gather up and stop. Next apply light pressure with the reins and take one step back. Position his nose in the direction you are going to turn by pulling lightly on the inside rein as you back up, and move him around using outside leg pressure. Be very smooth with your hands: no jerking or snatching. Horses may want to lug in this maneuver. You need energy to make this rollback sharp, use spurs if needed, or slap his shoulder with the loose end of your split reins.

With practice, we need to do rollbacks at all three gaits. It is very important that you leave the rollback at the same pace you went into it. If I start the rollback at the trot, I leave the rollback at the trot. If I start at the lope, I leave at a lope, and so on.

We don't want any hesitation after his front feet hit their mark. We need him to learn to pull with his front feet and push with his hind feet.

Remember to stay in the middle of the horse. Don't lean forward or toward the direction you want to go. You don't want to pull this horse out of position with your weight. Keep steady backward pressure with your hands to keep him in control and collected. As soon as you have reversed directions, use your voice and legs to encourage him to accelerate out of the turn. Only do a couple of rollbacks in one session, or your horse will start to anticipate. Never let a horse get the upper hand, like any herding animal does instinctively.

Horsemanship Accomplished

Remember to be consistent and ask your horse in the same manner each time. Consistency lends itself to speed and sharpness. By being consistent, you build good habits for both you and your horse. Repetition develops confidence between you and your horse, and when you feel you are ready to go to your first event, you will not be nervous. Confident horses know what to expect of us and so do we of them. A horse has a simple mind; he thinks only about eating, drinking, sleeping, and hopefully getting to do something new and fresh when you saddle him.

The human is more apt to be thinking about trivial things. We have a lot going on in our lives, which can allow us to make mistakes. Really try to focus; leave personal problems outside the practice pen and pay attention to being a good leader for your horse. Once your horse is started right, there is really no reason for him to make a mistake unless you make a mistake. Ninety percent of the time, problems or lack of proper execution with your horse are pilot errors. Most mistakes will need to be addressed by looking at what is going on in the saddle. Although this is sobering, it is true.

The maneuvers you need are the foundation for a well-educated horse, willing to respond in a split second. A well-broke horse doesn't happen overnight. I think it takes between two to four years to get there. If you cut corners now, you will definitely see problems crop up in your barrel racing.

Never ram and jam and expect a young horse to absorb it all. Shortcuts make horses mad because they can't understand what you really want.

You have to have a good attitude for your horse to have one. Think about your program before you go to the practice pen and be willing to address the problem at hand. If you avoid issues or weak spots with your training, they will only get worse at the most embarrassing moments. Go to that arena or pasture with a plan in mind. Every time

8

you go out and ride, decide what you are going to be doing, and set goals for the day.

Vary your horse's training program. Don't get in a rut, doing the same thing day after day. You will bore him and you will start seeing resistance or indifference. Do lots of different things on your horse: work cattle, trail ride, or rope. Vary his life; so whenever you discover his favorite event, he'll be prepared to go to work and be successful for you. Do remember that no matter how hard you work or how much you want this special horse to be the best horse you have ever tried, not every horse can or wants to be a barrel horse. If that's the case, go on and find a new horse that wants to do whatever you ask of him. As the saying goes, Great horses make great horsemen. Keep this in the back of your mind when a horse is not training well.

The Barrel Pattern

It doesn't matter how old your champion horse is, when you start him on barrels, techniques are the same. Whether he is four or twelve, the training is the same.

I always say, "Practice perfect and create good habits." Habits are formed through repetition. Of course we want them to be good habits, so know your job and ask your horse the same way every time. When you get consistent your horse will get consistent and gain confidence in you. The speed it takes to be a champion barrel horse will come automatically.

Getting Started

Let's start by setting up a normal-sized barrel pattern. Doing this will give your horse some time to relax in between barrels and feel rewarded until we ask them to turn again. The Women's Professional Rodeo Association regulation pattern calls for 90 feet between the first and second barrel and 105 feet from second to third. If I have the option, I like to set the barrels up out in an open pasture with good footing instead of in the confinements of an arena. It keeps a horse hunting the barrels rather than relying on a fence. Pay attention to the ruts that will develop from going around a barrel several times a day and try to keep them filled in as often as possible.

I start my horses out in a dee ring snaffle and German martingale, which is a training device that helps the horse control his head. I try to not use a tie down if at all possible, but there are some individuals that may need one. Experiment to see what makes your horse happy and turning the barrels with little or no resistance. The objective is to keep his head as quiet and steady as possible. We don't want the horse's head coming up; we want him bending his nose toward his side and shoulder and then holding his head in that nice, steady position till we ask him to straighten out. In barrel racing, every time a horse resists you, you lose tenths of a second.

So, use whatever headgear accomplishes this best. Unfortunately, only about 50 percent of horses running barrels don't require any type of additional training aids.

Adjust your reins before you start, because if your reins are too long you may get behind your horse when he leaves a barrel, or be late in correcting a problem that has occurred. If your reins are too long, your hand position may end up too far to the side, too high in the air, or down by your knee as you try to make contact with the horse's mouth. This can cause you to lean into the turn, which puts a horse off balance. When you come off the first barrel, you won't be able to reach down the left rein as far as you need to, leaving your hand in the middle of the rein. If your hand is too close to the center of the rein during a turn, your horse can't bend his head toward the barrel. Shorter reins allow your hand to be properly positioned down the inside rein, toward the bit, as soon as you come off the first barrel. In your turn, you want the outside rein loose, the inside rein snug, so your horse can tip his nose the direction you're asking him to turn through directional reining.

Rule of thumb is when your horse is relaxed and standing in a normal position, the reins should be about three inches in front of the saddle horn. It could be helpful to put tape on each side of the reins where you want your hand to be during a turn. This will help with consistency, which means so much to your horse. Reaching too far down the rein can cause you to lose control of your horse's hindquarters so you need to find that perfect place and mark it. About six inches from the center of your rein should be just about right.

Keeping your horse calm at the beginning of the pattern takes some concentration on your part. If you watched my National Finals Rodeo runs in 2000, you can see how quietly and calmly my horses walked down the alley. Control of this situation starts right here in your practice pen from day one.

Facing the barrel pattern, about 100 feet from the first barrel is considered the hot zone. It is where the pressure is applied later on in the training. Right off the bat you need to learn to relax. Sit deep in your saddle and keep your shoulders and head in line with your hips and the heels of your boots. Line up with the third barrel, spread your hands apart and guide your horse to the pocket of the first barrel. Make sure you hold your hands ten or twelve inches apart. This guarantees you will have complete control over both sides of your horse. Once you have established the speed you want, try to change to a loose rein. Avoid pulling on him or making contact with the bit, which numbs and desensitizes his mouth. Because of this freedom, when you get to the barrel and then sit, he will slow down on his own. If you hold the reins tight all the way to a barrel, his mouth will become numb, and he will brace on the bit and not respond to you. Turn him loose and then take hold again when it is time to slow down and turn the barrel.

The area ten feet from the barrel is called the pocket; it is the space between the barrel and the point that your horse starts turning the barrel. The pocket is important because it helps your horse to keep running around the barrel and to finish right by the barrel, so that it is easy to get ready for the next barrel turn.

Line up with the third barrel for a perfect approach to the first barrel.

Your approach to the first barrel should follow a path that lines up across from the third barrel; gradually arc toward the first barrel pocket. Look out in front of your horse and focus on where you want to end up. Guide him with your hands, eyes, and legs.

About ten feet out, sit down in your saddle and say "easy," and collect your horse with both reins. Always have four to five feet between the barrel and your horse's head at the point your horse enters the turn. When your horse's nose is even with the barrel, drop your outside rein and hold your saddle horn, pushing yourself down into your saddle. Sitting deep, lightly squeeze with your inside leg and bend his rib cage around the barrel.

Keep your rein hand above the swells of your saddle and your eyes and chin up; look beyond your horse's nose and watch him go around the barrel. As soon as his hip passes the barrel heading toward the next one, reach up with your outside hand, straighten his head and move him over with your outside leg preparing for the next barrel. Do this immediately no matter what size the barrel pattern you are running, always being ready for the second barrel pocket and turn.

In the pocket.

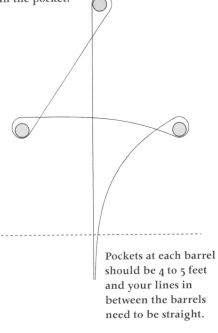

Pockets at each barrel should be 4 to 5 feet and your lines in between the barrels need to be straight.

Where do we accelerate? This is just as important as getting slowed down to collect; you have to show your horse when and where to add speed. Two-thirds around the barrel, start to encourage your horse by kissing or making a sound that will make him accelerate. Very slowly, inch by inch, give him a loose rein, and without moving your upper body forward, start using your legs to encourage him to start running off the barrel. When his hip passes the barrel, reach up the rein with your outside hand (the hand that was on the horn) and guide him in a straight line to the next barrel pocket. When you leave the first barrel, make sure you reach down the outside rein deep toward the bit to ensure you have a loose outside rein when turning the next

Drive straight to the pocket in the run position.

two barrels. This enables the horse to bend his head and arc his body in the shape of a barrel. This type of turn is the easiest and safest way for a horse to turn a barrel on any type of ground.

Every time you go through the barrel pattern, do it the same way that you will be doing it in competition even if you are at the walk. Our intuitive mind is the basis of habits. Once you have learned a sequence of movements through repetition, you don't need to think about each increment. When our thinking mind tries to run our body, it does a very poor job. Your muscles will not move as precisely as you need them to. Practice perfect so that when it comes time for competition, nothing changes no matter how many people are watching or how nervous you feel. Remember you are the leader—always practice perfect no matter what speed you are going.

Be very balanced and centered on your horse; if you lean, your horse will have to compensate for it. Keep your shoulders even with his ears and keep your hands over the swells of your saddle, your elbows in, with thumbs facing each other or slightly up, and keep you chin up and eyes looking directly ahead. Use your saddle horn in the turns to push yourself down in the saddle seat. Be light with your hand when you reach up to have two hands on the reins between barrels, trying never to balance on the reins. Grip with your thighs and keep your heels down. Staying in good physical shape will help your riding skills. Lots of time spent in the saddle, or as the old-timers said, lots of wet saddle blankets, makes better riders.

To relax or reward your horse, lean back and pet him on the rump, instead of leaning forward, which normally tells a horse to accelerate. When you lean back to pet your horse, your knees release off his sides, which means "good" in horse language.

I would walk the pattern for fifteen minutes for two weeks, then start speeding it up.

Speeding It Up

Now ride the pattern at the trot and lope. Here's where you will teach the horse where to slow down and where to accelerate. Slow him down, or collect or shorten his stride, right at the barrel so his hindquarters come up under him; this will bring his hind leg, or pivot leg, forward

Here, the outside rein is too tight, tipping the horse's head away from the barrel. The rider's feet don't hang directly below her hips. Avoid poor form.

Teach the horse to slow
down right at the barrel.

under his belly to start
the turn. Do this the
same way on all three
barrels, making sure
you are consistent in
your commands.

The next technique
really makes sense to a horse. If you choose to trot to the first barrel
and walk around it, then you need to trot to the second and third and
walk around them as well. Repeat your approach for all barrels; don't
single out one barrel and treat it differently, especially when you're
starting a horse. I see a lot of riders go slow to the first barrel, then go a
little faster to the second, then gallop to the third and run home. Avoid
this type of practice; the horse will be confused and won't become
consistent as quickly when it comes time to run him to all three. Consistency and repetition are key to a solid foundation. Remember, slow
work is as important for you and your horse as speed runs.

Let's talk about approaching a barrel and where the horse's body
should be in reference to the barrel. You want to be parallel to the barrel at the beginning of the turn. You must ride with two hands on the
reins to control both sides of your horse and insure you start the turn
parallel to the barrel. Your legs will control his hind end, and this will
help you control his shoulder. The shoulder goes hand in hand with
the hip. When I come up to the first barrel, I sit, say "easy," and slow
down. I never allow a horse to put his hip closer or farther away from
the barrel than his shoulder is. If you allow this now at slow speeds,
it will be accentuated at faster gaits and pose problems with the turn.
Also he won't have much push from his hindquarters; his powerhouse
loses efficiency if his hips are not directly underneath him.

I've seen a lot of riders let their horses lock their hips or bring them
closer to the barrel than their shoulder. The hip is then pushed to the
inside, and the shoulders lock up. The result? Horses raise their head,

drop their shoulder, and hit the barrel at the beginning of the turn. You want the hip to follow your horse's shoulders and stay in line with his body to maximize balance, strength, and quickness.

To start your approach, follow the line of sight. Keep your horse straight, hips and shoulders even. As you trot around the barrel, the hips may feel slightly out of line with the shoulder. This is okay—it will push the horse's front end around the barrel. When the hip has passed the barrel, move your horse over with your outside hand and outside leg. Trot to the second barrel, sit, and slow down parallel to the barrel, making sure the shoulder and the hip are the same distance from the barrel. If your horse did not slow down, completely stop—straight. Don't let him stop with his hip facing the third barrel or the finish line, which leads to later turn problems. If he stops with the hip locked up under him, correct him, move him back into the proper alignment, and make him relax and be still there for about the count of three.

To keep him parallel to the barrel, use your legs. Your legs do 80 percent of the work to control your horse. Your hands add 10 percent and your voice does 10 percent. Sit and slow down or stop at the same place every time. When I ask my horse to walk forward, I release the outside rein, keep my inside hand just above the swells or horn, and ask him to move forward by squeezing with my inside leg, not my body or release

of the rein hand. This is the same position of posture and rein hand that I want to maintain during a speed run. I keep my hand still and guide my horse around the barrel, and I do not release his head too

Example of your horse's hip locked up under himself prior to turning the second barrel. You will correct this with your inside leg.

early. If I do, my horse will start running in the turn too soon and come off wide, or straighten his body and hit the barrel leaving. So, hold him in the turn with a light tension of the inside rein until your body passes by the barrel heading toward the next one.

When you have gone through all three barrels, reward your horse with loose reins and a rub. When you get back to the starting point, always turn around and face the pattern and sit there for a moment. Leave him alone. If you get nervous in this hot zone, he'll get nervous right along with you. If you ride a nervous individual, remember to always take and release with your reins, take big long breaths, relax your legs, walk him forward, then stop and pet him. Walk him forward, stop him, and stand for the count of ten, letting him know that this area is a good place to stand and relax. This takes time and patience, if you do not have time in a particular session, walk a large circle before you repeat the pattern.

Before I ever lope a horse through the barrel pattern, I teach him to lope a single barrel. Set a barrel out in the middle of the arena. Lope a large 50-foot circle around the barrel, several rotations. When the horse feels comfortable, approach the barrel like normal, turn it, and go back out to the large circle. Train for success. Give him confidence that he can do this and that it's easy. It's important that you teach him to lope around one barrel first before you ever expect him to lope through the entire pattern and be comfortable doing it.

Notice your tracks around each barrel when you finish each lope through. On freshly groomed ground, you can use your tracks to learn a lot about what you are doing right or wrong. Look at your approach, evaluate your pocket size, and notice where you're leaving a barrel and how you're moving over or approaching the next one. The tracks tell the whole story. When you really need to know how you and your horse are doing, look at your tracks.

I get asked at our clinics a lot about leads going into barrels, especially the first. When I first start loping a horse around a barrel pattern, I want him to start out in the correct lead. I give myself some room to circle, and ask him to lope. If he picked up the correct lead, then I go on to the first barrel; if not, I slow to a trot and circle till I get on the correct lead.

Position his head toward the barrel immediately when you start to lope toward the barrel, as you did at the walk and trot. Halfway across to the second barrel, slow him down to a trot and then ask him to lope, using your outside leg to achieve the correct lead. Continue on if he is in the proper lead. If not, slow down to a trot and go around the second barrel, then ask him to lope in the correct lead to the third. If he misses the lead, slow down halfway and ask again. If he fails again, trot the barrel and lope home. Before doing the barrel pattern again, work on the lead commands and make sure he is listening and accomplishing them. If you were to keep trying to pick up leads in the barrel pattern, on the straight line you are going to frustrate this horse. Most problems need to be fixed without the barrels, when you and the horse are not worrying about the next turn which comes up fast.

Keep him moving once you have finished the pattern in practice. Don't make him stop and stand facing the pattern every time. When your horse starts getting tired, you can stop and let him rest facing the barrel pattern. Use common sense and do what is best for your horse. Don't put him into a situation where he can't win.

It will not take long before your horse will start knowing what you're going to do; some get aggressive and nervous now. The horse anticipates the start and usually makes a mistake on one of the three barrels. Give him a break from barrel work for thirty days and then start back. You have plenty of time to train your horse. He is not going to really get good and consistent until three or four years of training.

After I've taught my horse a few times to change leads between the first and second barrels, I quit worrying about it. I start letting my horse figure it out on his own. If I help him approach the barrel, have the perfect size pocket every time, slow him down at the right place, use my legs properly, and keep myself very still, he'll figure out how to use his legs accordingly. This understanding comes with conditioning and practicing our horsemanship maneuvers. If your horse is properly conditioned and well broke, you will have fewer problems with leads.

Horses want to work hard, they want to do right, and they can, as long as you do your job as a well-educated leader. I know this is your goal because you are taking the time to read this book.

After loping the pattern and finishing up for the day, I just walk the pattern and really relax my horse. I still practice perfect, though. I don't slop through it because I don't expect him to slop through it. I slow him down before his turn, shorten his stride, use my inside

Approach the first barrel with the head slightly tipped.

leg, put my hand on the horn—just like I would do if I was competing. Move him over, and then walk across to your second barrel with
a loose rein. I can't stress the loose rein part enough. Riders want to
keep contact with their horse's mouth when they go slow. Then when
they add speed to the run and turn their heads loose, the horse has
never felt this freedom before. He doesn't know what to do and has
no confidence in you, because you have changed your routine. They
usually act like they have never seen a barrel before. Really work on
being consistent; everything you do slow has to represent what you
will be doing fast.

Exercises

Many of the questions I get about finished barrel horses deal with
keeping that winning edge we've been working toward, questions that
all relate to a horse's sharpness during execution.

Over time, with lots of repetition, even human athletes loose sharpness. In this section I want to focus on the things you can do to keep
your barrel horse sharp throughout his entire career and hold that
winning edge. There are seven exercises that I do with my horses to

keep both my horse and me sharp and engaged in barrel racing. Both my horse and I get bored easily. These exercises are designed to keep both you and your horse enthusiastic and in the game.

These exercises keep horses relaxed and mentally level. I do them once a week; I do most of them at the trot in sets of three. The goal is to remove boredom, take away anticipation, fix some problems, and prevent problems in the future. They are all very simple, but you really need to think and focus when you are doing them, because you are the leader of your horse.

Choose a bit with plenty of bend and flex, like the dee ring snaffle and a German martingale, with a cavesson.

Practice perfect. Line up every time with the third barrel and adjust your reins to a comfortable length, leaving ten to twelve inches between your hands, and long enough so you sit upright. Remember, you need to be focused and thinking this entire time. Use all the pieces of the puzzle to do these exercises properly. The first five exercises use your regular barrel pattern. The last two exercises will require cones or tires. During all these exercises, use two hands on the reins all the way around the barrel to keep your horse from cueing off the dropping of the outside rein at the beginning of the turn. Practice for your horse 50 percent of the time and for you 50 percent of the time. Riding with two hands on the reins throughout the whole turn has never benefited me in competition. It has been done with success on a few horses, but we need to look at the majority when make decisions like this.

Reverse Pattern

For the first exercise take your horse to the other barrel first. If you normally run right, go left. This exercise will keep your horse running down the middle of the pen to prevent him from taking away the pocket on the first barrel. It enhances getting him moved over after he leaves the first barrel and really helps to position him properly for the second barrel.

Take this horse the opposite way, tip his nose in the direction you want him to go, and practice perfect. Ten feet out sit, say "easy," collect your horse to a walk, apply inside leg pressure, sit still, and let your horse turn the barrel. Keep your chin up, your elbows in, and let this horse work. When my body passes the barrel, I squeeze with my outside leg and kiss to him to pick up to a trot and go on to the next barrel pocket.

When you are done, reward this horse, let him relax, and remember the principles of the hot zone. Do this in increments of three.

Three Turns, One Direction

The second exercise involves turning the barrels all in the same direction; go to the first barrel, then the third barrel, and back to the second barrel.

You will be turning to the left around all three barrels at the trot in a triangle pattern. Do this three times to the left and three times to the right. This will help this horse be fluid in his turns and makes him really finish the turn before going on to the next. It helps take anticipation and boredom out of the run and helps you and your horse communicate.

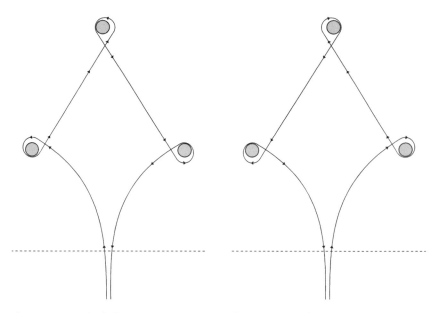

The pattern to the left.   The pattern to the right.

Again, practice perfect, doing all the things you normally do. Sit, "easy," collect to a walk or slower trot, sit yourself upright in the saddle, take his nose, sit still while completing the turn, move him over, and go to your next barrel and turn it in the same direction. Make sure your horse is bending properly, moving off your leg and keeping a steady cadence around the barrels. Make sure you have the correct size pocket, and be smooth and steady.

Do this around all three barrels, turning them in the same direction. Repeat it three times, and then ride the other direction. Maintain your hands, use your legs to bend the rib cage, and don't interfere with his forward motion.

Twice Around

In this next exercise you are going to circle the barrel twice. This keeps your horse from starting to run too soon in the turn, which happens a lot. This is how you correct it. It helps you to know where your horse is at all times, all the way through the turn. I use one hand most of the time with this exercise because it is easy to do it with two hands. Manage your horse with your legs and don't reach up with that outside hand like you normally would to move him over after the first time around. Just hold him there in the turn and drive with your legs to turn the barrel again.

When your body passes that barrel the second time around, reach up and move him over and go straight to the pocket. Circle the second and third barrel twice and come straight home just like you do in competition.

The Funnel Barrel Exercise

The next exercise uses six or eight barrels and gets a horse to really look for a barrel. They start paying attention to where a barrel is; it also makes them finish their turns. If they are really nervous, it slows them down and makes them relax and think. Because you are making so many turns around the barrel, it takes their minds off running. It also gets a horse really moving over off the first barrel. Do this exercise at a walk, trot, and lope in both directions, three times. When I lope this exercise, I use my competition bit.

Space the two lines of barrels 50 feet apart, along the sides. Space the first pair 20 feet apart, the second set 50 feet apart, the third set 80 feet apart, and, if you have a fourth set, make them 110 feet apart.

Your pockets and turn are just like a normal barrel turn. You can practice with two hands all the way through the turn at a walk or trot.

When I do it at a lope, I use one hand in the turn. It does not matter which end you start at or what side you start with. I do it every which way to keep it fun. The diagrams below will show you the different ways to use this exercise.

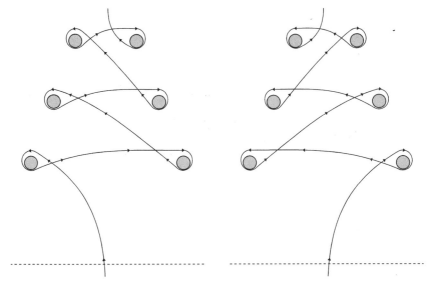

You can start at either end and from any direction and trot or lope the pattern.

Single Barrel with Cones

I use this for several purposes. Use it when you are just starting a horse and want to teach him the basics of turning a barrel before you ever lope the whole pattern. It is also great for a nervous horse that wants to speed up when he starts the turn. I use this exercise to help me make sure I am using my legs properly and determine if I am sitting still in my turns and not leaning too much in either direction. Any of these rider problems cause my horse to lose momentum and break down to a trot when he leaves the turn, or he may crossfire behind, meaning that he'll be on the wrong lead with the inside hind leg.

Set four or six cones up about 40 feet from the barrel. It does not have to be exact; just go with a distance that makes you comfortable. The cones will allow you to lope the parameter, keeping a constant round circle.

Start thinking about the turn and gradually guide your horse to the pocket of the turn; turn the barrel. I will use two hands the first time I try this exercise and one hand the second time. Keep his nose tucked to the center of the circle and your weight in the outside stirrup. With quiet hands and your chin up, lope the perimeter five or six times to get your horse relaxed and comfortable. If your horse is one of those speed demons, lope the perimeter a little longer until he settles down.

Approach the barrel just as you normally would, with your pocket in mind. When you enter the inside of the cones, sit, squeeze lightly with your inside leg, release the inside rein, and turn the barrel once. Then release the inside rein slowly, reach up with your outside rein hand, squeeze with both legs, and come out the next cone over from where you entered. Nice and smooth. There should be no dropping of the hind lead, and he should not break down to a trot.

The next time you go in to turn the barrel, make sure you use a different entrance cone. We are creatures of habit; change it up to alleviate that anticipation in your horse. Sit, squeeze, relax, chin up, and come back out one cone over. Again, nice and smooth. Maintain a lope.

Stop, back up, and then reverse direction. You want him to respond immediately and go the other direction in the correct lead.

REVIEW The cones will help you know where you are. Concentrate on keeping quiet hands. Tip the nose and hold it. Your hand should not move. Manage your turns with your legs. Focus on him keeping his hind lead. Keep it smooth. When he enters the interior of the cones, you don't want him to speed up. Everything is fluid and relaxed. You can use any bit that gives you bend and plenty of control, usually the bit you compete in. This exercise will tell you if you are not using enough leg pressure, or if you dropped your inside rein hand below the swells of the saddle; is your weight in the outside stirrup; do you have

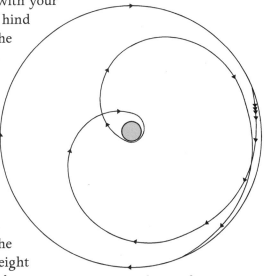

Follow the arrows for a perfect turn.

enough pressure on the inside rein; are you leaning forward too much? This is your checklist. Run through it in your head as you try the exercise. If you do anything wrong, then your horse will trot or crossfire when he leaves the barrel pattern.

Cones and the Pattern

The last exercise will require cones positioned throughout the pattern. Cones will help you and your horse with precision by helping you judge the distance needed for correct pocket size. You will use them to help you move your horse over where you need to be and maintain those nice, straight lines required for fast finish times.

Your first cone should be placed three feet from the first barrel, between you and the barrel. This cone helps you maintain that four- to five-foot pocket size. Place it so it will not interfere with your turn when leaving the barrel. The cones are not meant to create an obstacle course; they are meant as guides to get you consistent and where you need to be at all times during your run.

Your second cone will be two feet away from your barrel, on the inside of your turn. The third will be placed about one foot away from the barrel, on the back side. This placement means that as we go around the barrel, we gradually get closer and closer.

The fourth cone will be positioned to help you move over and prepare for your second turn. Place it one-third of the way across, between your first and second barrels, to help you move over quickly to be properly lined up for your second barrel pocket, advancing in a straight line.

Set up cones around the second and third barrel like you did for the first. Position one cone one-third, and another two-thirds of

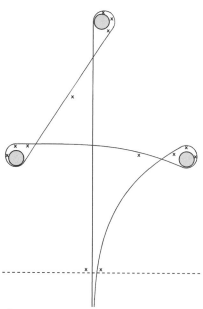

Placement of cones or tires is indicated by an x.

the way to your third barrel, to help prevent bowing off the second barrel, creating a straight line to your third barrel.

Focus on this part, because we know that the shortest distance between two points is a straight line. I don't want to be wide off the second barrel, creating an arc to the third barrel, which makes too much pocket on the third barrel. Your horse's hip will not be up under him for that quick, powerful turn. Use cones to get in the habit of going in a straight line.

Most riders will find that these cones will really cause you some difficulty the first time or two through. It is worth the effort to set them up once a week. Anytime we are not moving forward on a very straight line, we lose momentum, as well as add distance to the pattern, which will add precious tenths of a second to our final time.

Now that you are all set up, trot to the barrel and walk around it, staying near the cones. Changing your gait from a trot to a walk puts a lot of rate in your horse. The only horses that I do not do transitions on are ones that want to slow down too soon. In this case, do fewer transitions and try speeding up where the horse wants to slow down. Remember to ask your horse to accelerate as your body is passing the barrel heading toward the next barrel. He should start trotting again right where you'd expect him to start running during competition. Do it three times, and then change the pace. This time lope to the barrels and trot around them. Again, the variation in gaits accentuates the rate factor. Do this three times. Then gallop to the barrels and lope around them.

Practice perfect every time you go through the barrel pattern. Speak to your horse, collect him evenly with both hands, and make the transition between the gaits very smooth.

Always keep in mind that you are the leader. You're the one that's teaching this horse sharpness. If he makes a mistake, you probably caused it. You need precision and focus. Really concentrate while you're doing these exercises, so you and your horse will get the most out of them.

Because barrel racing is a precision event, you must know where your horse is in relation to the barrel. No matter what you're doing, you have to be precise. Don't stop too early or too late. Don't be too close or too far out from the barrel. Keep your hands in the proper position on the reins. Make sure you are using your legs. Do everything just like in competition; nothing should change. Practicing perfect requires perfect practice.

At my clinics I see so much improvement in both horse and rider after we have done all of these exercises. It gets you out of that humdrum routine that we get stuck in. This is one of the ways to keep both horse and rider enthused with their jobs.

At the end of your exercises, go through your normal pattern. Then return to the hot zone, get off, and uncinch your horse. Anytime you release pressure is a reward, whether it is loose reins, getting off, or uncinching. The whole point of these exercises is to keep your horse wanting to barrel race of his own free will and happy to do it. Then the sport is enjoyable for both of you.

CHAPTER 10

Champion Mental Game for Horse and Rider

Nothing can stop the man with the right mental attitude from achieving his goal; nothing on earth can help the man with the wrong mental attitude.

—W. W. ZIEGE

I F ALL the parts of the champion puzzle are in place and working effectively and you still experience difficulties, look to the mental aspects of competition and you will surely find the problem. The right mental attitude makes the difference in anything we do.

In preparing for competition, three areas are key. The first is in physical skills, the second in technical skills, and the third in psychological skills. All three of these categories are required for both rider and horse in champion level success. We've covered the first and second categories in the preceding pages. Now let's work on that last area: psychological skill, better known as the mental game.

How often have we watched ourselves or another rider leave the arena as if to say, "I don't know what I was thinking? I just lost my head. I just choked after he blew the first barrel." That response comes from lack of mental preparation. Mental preparation is just as essential to the success of any athlete as physical preparation. Just as we have trained the muscles of our champion horse, we must train our own mind to be relaxed, focused, and positive. Practice each task until you are comfortable with it, and then practice it in your mind to help perfect it.

At the 1988 Winter Olympics held in Calgary, Canada, I won two gold medals. Shown here with the silver medalist, Martha Josey, and bronze medalist, Charmayne James.

The following information is designed to help you prepare mentally for competition. Practice your mental game with the same intensity and seriousness that you practice the physical and technical parts of your program. Use these techniques before competition, when you are unable to ride or work your horse, and you are alone. By practicing these techniques, you will feel more relaxed, confident, and prepared when you compete.

The first step is to observe; go and watch the best barrel racers execute runs. You need mental images of perfect runs to build from during mental preparation. At this time I want to warn you of watching videotapes of yourself too much. I have seen riders morally defeat themselves by criticizing their runs. Instead, watch your run three or four times, then decide what you want to work on in your next practice sessions.

How do you prepare for a specific event? When you get to the competition, go observe the arena and its environment. Check the ground, check the alley, and check where the electric timer will be and how far down the first barrel is from the entrance gate of the arena. Get a visual image of where you will be competing. Take that image back to a quiet space and start preparing your mental game. Ask yourself: Was the ground hard, deep, or slick? Were there banners on the back side of the first barrel flapping in the wind? Was the gate in a difficult place to get set up properly? Such factors are essential pieces to mental preparation. If there are challenges that will make execution difficult, now is the time to make your plan for how to avoid or get around them. Tape that banner down; walk your horse around the arena so he gets a feel for the footing, lay out your plan for how to get through that gate or down the alley to be lined up properly. These practices also avoid problems and, very often, injury to both horse and rider.

Now that you have that mental image, take it to your trailer or wherever you can have some quiet time. Even if you have to wear headphones or earplugs, it is imperative to be alone in a quiet space. Now imagine yourself coming down the alley and make a game plan. Tell your body what you are going to do with that difficult ground, challenging gate, or whatever difficulties you will be faced with. Anticipate those problems so that if or when they occur you know how to handle them. By doing this you will learn how to refocus and stay relaxed in a run. If you have to make a run without the liberty of identifying the challenges firsthand, try to imagine it the best that you can. Plan how you will handle your run successfully, ignore distractions, maintain concentrated focus, and regroup during problems.

Get comfortable, close your eyes, sit up straight, and relax with some deep breaths. This will reduce your heart rate and help with concentration. Envision yourself high above the arena. If you were able to check out the area firsthand, remember and visualize all the aspects you noted.

If you have difficulty performing a certain task, concentrate and visualize yourself doing it over and over till it becomes perfect and easy. Picture yourself doing it slowly at first. Picture yourself practicing it at home, at other races, and finally visualize today's arena. Now speed up your imaginary runs. Visualize your fingers, arms, and legs. Picture every detail from the saddle during perfect execution. Keep taking deep breaths so your mind and body feel no fear. If you take short breaths, your mind thinks you are in trouble, and your body tenses up. Your horse feels this through your hands, seat, and legs. Better to breathe deeply, so your mind tells your body all is okay.

Once you have solved the challenges and are mentally executing these well, visually incorporate them into your entire run. Elite athletes have long advocated this component of mental preparation. The ability to mentally stimulate your brain to see, hear, smell, and sense a preferred outcome strengthens and fine-tunes the pathways to body memory and habits. Picture that perfect run from start to finish over and over again. You may even physically tighten your muscles or move your body while you mentally visualize that run. Golfers and bowlers repeat their arm and hand motions until perfect. Try it. Position your hands correctly on your reins; use your inside leg; visualize whatever you need to do properly. Do this repeatedly until it all flows together quickly and perfectly.

The use of positive self-talk is important to mental preparation. Coaches try to motivate their players before a game with inspiring talks in the locker room. In barrel racing, you have to act as the coach and player. Remind yourself that the winning run is yours for the taking. If you are positive and remind yourself of what you have done to prepare, you are using positive thinking to psych yourself up. With this comes confidence and success. Here are a few examples of thoughts to repeat to yourself:

"I can and will make a perfect run."
"I have trained my mind, body, and horse to succeed."
"I know how to confront and correct any problem that arises."
"Just do what you know how to do."
"Feel my horse and respond to it."

If you are unsure whether your talks are positive, just ask yourself if you would say that thought out loud to inspire a friend. If you wouldn't dream of telling Betty Lou, "I am afraid Wildfire is going to bulldoze that first barrel again today," don't think it to yourself EVER when getting mentally prepared. Instead say, "If Wildfire drops that shoulder, I know how I will handle that problem. I know how to overcome it and go on to the next barrel and make a winning run." Turn over your control from your thinking mind to your body.

Most of the time, competitors beat themselves before they ever enter the gate. It takes practice, persistence, and patience to learn how to stay positive in stressful situations.

Fear and nervousness come from the unknown. An example would be if you are riding a new horse and you do not know what to expect. Always test the runs at home and jackpots, so you can learn what to expect from this horse. When you become comfortable with your horse, the nervousness will go away. You will still have the feeling of a fast heartbeat, but will know what to expect.

Another common situation occurs when we get to the barrel race and see someone more successful entered. How many times have you thought, "Dang. There's Smokin Sally. I hoped she wouldn't come today. I may as well load up and go home now." This is a competition, yes, but ultimately in barrel racing we are competing against ourselves and a clock. Strive not to beat another competitor, but your last performance. Focus on being better each time you compete.

Another mental hurdle will present itself in the form of the environment. Have you ever looked at the ground and said, "Geez. The ground is horrible, my horse hates hard ground"? Focus on the facts. Everybody who runs is going to have the same conditions. Focus on yourself and what you can do to overcome the challenge. If your horse slips, runs by, or you encounter another problem, be prepared to correct it and go on with your run. Many competitors let down mentally when the going gets tough; others become stronger, more determined, or more focused. How you respond when a problem happens is usually a direct result of self-talk. If you said, "Oh great, I knew he needed more set, why did I let him run by it?", chances are problems will continue and may worsen as you go. However, if you say to yourself, "There he goes on by. Get a hold of him, say 'easy,' and sit hard right now. Now get in position and smoke that third," you might salvage the run and stay in the money. Why? Because you didn't quit; you corrected a problem and kept riding. You positively talked yourself through a problem by focusing on what to do next. You turned a negative into a positive. Positive thinking will result in a positive outcome. Skip the self-sabotage and learn how to deal with problems effectively. Out of 200 competition runs each year, I can honestly say that I only make ten flawless ones. Do not sabotage your run by finishing before you're done with the third barrel or reach the finish line. If you anticipate the end, your mind thinks you're done and tells your body to relax and slow down. Finish the run from start to finish before you congratulate yourself. *Don't count your chickens before they hatch.*

The last point I would like to cover is a situation I have myself experienced and watched other riders experience often: knowing the difference between fear and adrenaline. Most people don't realize that all competitive performances run on "arousal," or "adrenaline." The key is knowing how much or how little arousal to allow your body to experience prior to that run. Every human and horse is different. Highly anxious performers need to focus on calming down and relaxing, while others need to "pump up," so to speak. There is no right or wrong way to mentally prepare for this. The key is to learn to maintain the proper level for you. I know some competitors like to listen to upbeat music or be around a person that is fun and tells you how good you and your horse are. You have to learn to maintain what level of arousal brings forth your best performance. This is also an area where you see many mismatches between rider and horse. Often the rider needs to stimulate arousal and the horse needs to relax. Each time you compete on a different horse, think, "What does this horse need from me?" Your mental game must mesh with your horse's mental game; this point makes mental preparation that much more important.

Often we are unable to practice barrel racing because of weather. Perhaps the horse does not need as much practice as we do. These off days are perfect times for mental practice. Do some light stretching at home, and practice your breathing and mental game. Learn how to make mental preparation as second nature as running that pattern perfectly. Make sure the last visualizations before your actual run are perfect and correct in every way. When you have mastered the mental game of competition, you will cross the finish line a winner.

PART SIX

Putting It All Together

*What counts is not necessarily the size of the dog in the fight—
it's the size of the fight in the dog.*

—Dwight D. Eisenhower

CHAPTER 11

Champion Run

You miss 100 percent of the shots you never take.

—WAYNE GRETZKY

Problems and Solutions

BEFORE WE end with a champion barrel run, here are some of the questions I receive about problems and how to correct them. We all have problems at one time or another. The funny thing about a problem is that it usually stems from a bad habit. As you know, bad habits are like a comfortable bed: easy to get into, but hard to get out of. This is why you hear me continually say, "Practice perfect." We don't want to get into bad habits, because they lead us down the path to problems. The best way to prevent problems from occurring is to be diligent about all the pieces of your champion puzzle.

The minute you put a halter on your horse, remember you are setting an example as a good leader. When you are in the saddle, focus and really pay attention to the details. When you feed, pay attention to the amounts. When your horse is shod, be there and pay attention to what the farrier is doing and keep records. When you saddle your horse, pay attention to how your saddle and tack fit. Watch your equine dentist so you will know when your horse's teeth need attention, and so on. Take an active role in every aspect of your champion program. Such attention will give you the ability

The Money Roll at the 2006 finals at San Angelo, Texas Rodeo. I won second place.

to identify and correct your own problems, before they are catastrophic. Diligence, dedication, and hard work will give you every tool you need to identify problems and their source. You will also be able to take the appropriate steps necessary to quickly correct them and keep making those champion runs.

So, here you are with a problem. Regardless of the nature of it, the first thing you need to look at is your overall puzzle. This is how we determine which pieces of the puzzle our problem is related to. Look back through the contents listed in this book and use it like a checklist. Evaluate your champion plan. Evaluate your champion horse. Evaluate your champion program and your champion tools. Then if everything else checks out, evaluate your champion execution and mental game.

Throughout the book, I give examples or tell you what role certain aspects play in the overall picture, like: "This exercise prevents your horse from taking away your pocket . . .", or, "This maneuver enhances your horse's sensitivity to leg pressure", or,

"This works well when your horse starts to bow off a barrel." The answers to the majority of your problems wait right here in the pages of this book.Start with your horse. Make sure all the pieces of your champion puzzle are in place. Ask yourself right away if the horse is hurting in some way. Many times these athletes won't show the normal clinical signs of pain. If your horse's performance is off or his attitude has drastically changed overnight, look to this piece of the puzzle first. Is the champion feed program in place? Are his feet properly shod? Have his teeth been floated? Is he well conditioned? Are you doing your horsemanship exercises enough? Within the pages of this book are the answers to how most problems originate. You spent the money on this book, so use it as a helpful tool and refer to it often. If you're not having problems, just refresh yourself to stay with those good habits that will prevent problems.

Let's talk about some of the most common problems I see and am asked about.

- I get lots of questions about problems with horses that will not come in the gate quietly, or how to resolve the issues of "arena sour" horses.
- I see a lot of barrels being knocked down because of pocket mismanagement.
- I get a lot of questions about horses that drop their shoulders and take away the rider's pocket, resulting in lots of knocked-down barrels.
- I also am frequently asked about horses that go into the barrel and then either sharply come back in a "V" shape, knocking barrels, or stall behind the barrel.
- I see horses coming off barrels wide, especially the third barrel.
- I see a lot of horses resisting the pressure of the bit or the rider's hands, gapping their mouths or tossing their heads.
- I see many riders with their reins way too long, or in need of a bit and headgear adjustment or change.
- I see riders leaning and getting their horses out of balance.
- I see horses that need more rate as they approach the barrels.

Let's address these one by one.

Questions and Answers

Gate Problems

QUESTION I am in need of some professional advice. I have a young mare, a five-year-old, that I have been trying to start myself. I purchased her as a long yearling and green broke her at 2 ½. She had not been handled before this. I sold her and repurchased her. The other owner turned her out and left her for three years without handling her at all. I started her over. She was doing great until I started her on the pattern. She knows the pattern, and if I rate her at the first barrel, she does fine. We are not running hard yet, but I have been asking her for a little more speed after the first turn. She used to walk right in the arena fine, but now she is rearing, lunging, and having a fit for about five minutes. If I sit quiet and keep insisting, she will drop her head and go in, but she is too much of a danger to herself and others to keep doing this. If I fight her, she fights back. So, for now I am only trail riding her. Now this problem is popping up whenever I take her out by herself. Could you give me some advice?

ANSWER As you can see in this example, this problem started in one place and spilled into another. This tells us it is not just barrel racing or asking for more speed that has caused this issue. Perhaps by not addressing the original cause, something has been overlooked. Start by checking all the pieces, making sure the puzzle is complete. In this case it clearly is missing something.

Is this horse healthy? Has her dental program been consistent? Is the equipment fitting properly? Did her owner check for injuries or things that could be causing discomfort or pain? These are the first things I would check out. Then I would ask the owner: Are you making barrel racing fun for your horse by varying her conditioning and exercise program? Are you practicing your horsemanship maneuvers on a regular basis; do you have problems with any of them? Are you staying relaxed and asking her in the correct manner that she understands? Are you riding up to the arena gate with just one hand on the reins, taking deep breaths, and staying relaxed?

Rule out as much as you can right off the bat. Go down that checklist. Then if all those pieces are in place, proceed to how you are handling this situation.

Focus on staying relaxed. When you go to enter your arena, keep forward motion at all times. Put one hand on the rein lightly and have the other nice and relaxed at your side or reaching back and touching her hip. Sit deep in your saddle so you are not leaning forward. Then if your mare puts on the brakes, coming to a screeching halt, and you are thrown forward before she rears, you will be ready for it.

Stay in the middle of your horse and be really calm, still, and balanced. Don't go to two hands on the reins until you need them; switch back and forth between hands or put them together in the middle of the reins. Keep her walking around before it is your turn to go and keep that forward momentum right into the arena. When you are done riding, face the barrel pattern and reward this mare by uncinching her, and pick up all four feet; for some reason it helps a horse to respect and trust you when you have control of her feet.

What you will notice is once something like this has happened a time or two, you will surely anticipate a recurrence. This is why it is important to figure out the problem right away. The more times they repeat, the more the behavior becomes a habit. Naturally, the frequent occurrence of this problem will cause you to tense up.

If this still doesn't help, get a long whip. When she rears or refuses to enter, tap her on the butt with the whip. You need to create pressure from behind so she will move forward. This will do two things to facilitate that forward motion. First, because you have to reach back to use the whip on her hip, that gets your weight off her front end, encouraging relaxation. Secondly, you'll need to use only one hand on the reins, which opens up the forward route.

You don't want her to run off from the whip, but you need to get that forward momentum back to get in the gate.

This approach also puts pressure on her when she is outside the arena. At this point the only pressure she has received has been inside the arena. Using the bat or having someone on the ground with a whip walking behind the horse will make the pressure more intense outside the arena. The horse will then seek the comfort of being inside. It is important to remove pressure anytime a horse makes a positive move, and in this case that would be as soon as she begins forward movement into the arena.

You also mentioned she is rearing up. When she goes up, she loses that forward momentum. She goes up first, then lunges, which tells me she wants to go forward, but feels some sort of heavy pressure with no way to get away from it. You have to find a way to release the pressure that is preventing her from moving ahead willingly.

Barn Sour

The other thing that should be addressed is the question of her being "barn sour" and not liking to leave her stablemates. Here is an example of another inquiry about this issue.

QUESTION I am training a two-year-old and have been working her for about four months. She has this thing where if I am riding with a friend, she cannot be separated. When she is, she will buck and rear to get back to them. I know this isn't very safe for me or the horse, so I was wondering how to get her to stop. If you could help out, that would be great. I don't want to be harsh, but I also know I have to be the boss. Thanks for your advice.

ANSWER A horse is a herd animal and naturally resists leaving the herd. Try this to alleviate the problem.

If you have the facilities, move her away from the barn or other horses she is with to a safe place where she cannot see them. This is a type of isolation, if you will. It will take about two weeks for her to adjust, but eventually she will find she can do things on her own without the others, including think.

This will help a barn sour horse become more independent and become dependent on you as her leader, friend, and keeper.

Furthermore, you have to demonstrate your leadership role with your horse from the beginning. A horse, if allowed, will be the leader. Ideally you get them to submit to *you* as a leader. In the barn sour case, the horse is showing no respect: she wants to return to the herd instead of be with you. A barn sour horse is spoiled and has been allowed to do her own thing.

Again, problems are born out of bad habits that we have gotten into or allowed our horses to get into. Often it is something very subtle that we are doing. Over time, it takes us down the road to a complicated and serious problem if not addressed immediately. These things can become dangerous. Your horse is counting on you to lead the way; otherwise, she will find her own way. This is why diligence and dedication to being a educated leader is vital, whether you are on her back or by her side.

Here is another example of an inquiry that deals with both of the last problems we talked about.

QUESTION I have a "soured" barrel horse that is making my life miserable. I can't get in the arena without a fight. He is rearing, spinning, and refusing the arena. He is an excellent barrel horse otherwise. I haven't competed on him for six months hoping that would help, but it was just the same old thing. Any help you could offer me would be great!

ANSWER Here we are with the same problems: resisting the gate, rearing, and spinning. The fix is the same in this case. If you will remember, I talked about how quietly my horses came down the alley at the National Finals Rodeo in 2000. I rode two horses at the NFR that year: Snazzy and Casey. Both of them did the same thing, each time. They entered the gate and proceeded up that alley quietly and calmly. They were focused on the task ahead of them, and this allowed me to focus and do my job well. It was clear that these horses were enjoying their job.

This is something that I get lots of acknowledgment for, and it amazes me that lots of people have difficulty here. I clearly have found how to avoid this problem through the years. This book can help with this. Go down that checklist and make sure everything is evaluated. Do your job to keep your horse liking what he is doing.

Hitting Barrels

Hitting barrels is probably the second most common area that riders have difficulty with. Lots of barrels get hit and knocked over for various reasons. The reasons can range from pocket mismanagement, allowing horses to drop their shoulders into their turns, or slicing or hitting barrels when coming back around them too sharply in a "V" shape. All of these problems stem from poor position or not setting our horses up properly to make that nice, smooth, fluid turn. We have to get the collection just right, position his nose with our hand in the perfect place, and shape him with our inside leg to create the perfect scenario when we get to the barrel. Here are some examples of riders frustrated about horses that drop their shoulders.

QUESTION I have a four-year-old that was patterned heavily before I got him. He really drops his shoulder on the first turn to the right. I just can't seem to catch him prior to him dropping it, he is just too quick. I can get him to turn correctly on other right turns, just not on the barrel pattern. I switched him to the left and I can get him to do his right turns better coming in at this different angle. What else can I do, and why can't I get him to turn properly when I switched him? Thanks for your help.

QUESTION I compete in reining in 4-H, and my horse tends to drop his shoulder and fall into his turns. Are there any basics I should add to help him get over this?

ANSWER When a horse drops his shoulder, the rider does not have complete control of the shoulder and hip. This is a very common problem, and I see it over and over again. As you head to your barrels, you need to get this horse's body in a position where he can use it when he gets there. Tip this horse's nose in the direction you are going to be turning. Remember when we talked about their nose indicating where their body will go? Well, this is a prime example.

If your horse is dropping his shoulder, his nose will be tipped out, away from the barrel. His rib cage will bend toward the barrel instead of curving around it. Getting the shoulder elevated, his nose tipped, and his rib cage moved away and curved by your inside leg pressure will eliminate this problem. It is a normal reaction to want to pull your horse's nose away from the barrel with your outside hand when this problem happens. Although it may seem like you are pulling him away from the barrel, you are actually forcing him into it. Instead, when you feel this happening, pick up on the inside rein and cross it over the neck. Get his nosed tipped into the barrel while applying heavy pressure or kicking with your inside leg. Remember we want him to move away from pressure, so use only the leg that will make him do this. A horse has to slow down early to drop a shoulder, so keep as much speed up as possible.

This is also a good time to implement the exercise we called "Counter-Arc at the Barrel." It is also a great time to review all the horsemanship exercises and make sure that you can move every body part without any stiffness or resistance.

Hitting Barrels Coming Out of Them

Let's move onto the problem of hitting barrels coming out of them. Here is a question from a professional rider who was experiencing this problem.

QUESTION My gelding Sporty that I purchased from you is just an exceptional athlete. I love everything about him and do win a lot on him. Lately, however, we are knocking down lots of barrels at rodeos. Don't get me wrong; we aren't crashing them, just barely skimming them when we come out. He turns so beautifully that I just can't identify the problem. Both my horse's technique and my own seem good. He does nothing wrong that I can see, and I am in the proper body position and staying still, letting him do his thing, which is usually smokin' his barrels. We still clock like nobody's business. It is so frustrating because he looks like he is going to just inhale the barrel and everything looks great, then we just barely tip them over as we're leaving. What is happening here? I just can't stop tipping these barrels for those big checks, and I am getting tired of hearing the announcer and entire crowd go "ahhhh," after a barrel goes down and costs me the win over and over again. You are the master, and I know nobody hits fewer barrels than you do. What do you think is going on here?

ANSWER This problem is usually created by one of two things: a pocket that is too large or letting him straighten his body and start running before he is done turning the barrel.

It only takes your horse a certain amount of space to complete a turn once you have locked him into it. For example, if the total area needed to turn your horse around a barrel without stalling or slowing down too much is six feet, four being your pocket and two for the barrel, and if you increase your pocket to six feet out, you can see that when you add that other foot or two it puts him right back over the top of the barrel.

Although often we see this in a much more exaggerated situation, this pro barrel racer's problem seems very subtle. Although it is subtle, it is enough to cost her at the pay window and take her confidence away.

If this happening on only your second or third barrel or more than one of them, look to your positioning. If you are not moving your horse over immediately and setting up the next turn by driving straight to it, this will increase your pocket and cost you precious time while you either run way out around the barrel or tip it over coming out. So, make sure your pocket is the correct size. Some horses don't require much pocket or room, especially the great ones. If you give them too much, they will either start hitting barrels coming out or waste too much time running around the barrel. Secondly, make sure you move your horse into position as soon as you leave each barrel and drive straight to the next pocket.

This would be a good time to get out those cones and really think about the exercises we called "The Cone Pattern" and "Twice Around."

The other possibility is that you allow him to straighten his body too soon by releasing your inside rein too much and leaning forward when you are only halfway around the barrel. Wait till your body passes the barrel, headed to the next one, before you really ask for speed and straighten up the horse's body. I bet you will find one of these two things to be causing this problem.

Leaving Barrels Wide

Here is a typical question from a barrel racer seeking help with a horse that is blowing off her turns wide.

QUESTION I have a seven-year-old mare that I have been working with for about three years. When I work with her at home, she will run an excellent pattern. Lately when I haul her, my first and second are good, but she comes off the third really wide. I changed directions, but then all my barrels were wide. I have made some bit changes and had her evaluated by a chiropractor and vet. Everything checked out fine. I would appreciate any advice you can give me.

ANSWER A horse will blow off any barrel wide for several reasons. She does not finish the turn before she starts running; see the previous answer. The exercise to use is circling the barrels two or three times. Perhaps you're not using enough outside leg pressure to move her over, or you are late getting to your outside rein hand up to straighten her head, or your reins are too long and you find yourself in the middle of them, not allowing the horse to bend her head the way you want her to go. Begin by doing some analysis. Look at rein length first, since it is easy and quick to assess. Your reins should be about three to four inches in front of your saddle horn when your horse is relaxed and you pick them up and make the curb chain come tight. You need to have between ten and twelve inches between your hands, or shoulder width, when going between the barrels. You need to reach down on your rein toward the bit where you need to be for getting the inside rein tight and the outside rein loose.

If your reins are okay, work on the other things that cause this problem.

When this happens on the third barrel, a horse and rider anticipating the run home can accentuate this problem. You know you smoked the first two barrels and want to get out of there and home as fast as possible. Unfortunately, the run home is just as important as the other parts of your run. Not running in a straight line is costing you precious time.

If you are not using enough outside leg or you are not getting to your outside rein fast enough, ride the exercise called "The Cone Pattern" more often. You will quickly find out if this is what is happening. If it is, this exercise will help you correct it and get your horse finishing his turns. The "Twice Around" exercise will also help. Another correction is to walk the pattern. As you finish your third barrel, turn, reach up with your outside rein, and apply pressure with your outside leg like you would normally do to move your horse over off the first barrel. Straighten her up, then counter-arc, hold this bend, and push her toward the first barrel. This really accentuates that process of moving over. If you are experienced and your horse is well broke, you can also do this at the lope.

Going by Barrels

In this case, the horse runs to the barrel and just goes right on by like he did not even see it. A multitude of things contribute to this scenario. Let's start with the simplest.

Rein length can play a factor, along with too much gag motion in the bit you are using. Your reaction time is too long if your reins are too long or your bit action too slow. Another very important thing to realize is that the more you pull on a horse, the more he wants to run. You hear about steer wrestling horses and racehorses doing this. If you have constant pressure on a horse's mouth, it is going to get numb and desensitized. You have got to turn these horses loose and then collect them back to a controlled speed.

You obviously do not have enough rate, collection, or slow down if your horse passes the barrel. Sit down in the saddle and say "easy, easy" and collect this horse. Collect him with two hands so you can control both sides of your horse's body. Exaggerate the collection by stopping him at each barrel, making sure he is parallel to the barrel, and then backing him up. If he moves a hip out when he stops or when he is backing, straighten him up with leg pressure. They have got to learn to gather themselves before the start of the turn. Remember when we worked our horse on the fence and asked him to stop by sitting, speaking, and then pulling on the reins. You need to refresh this horse's memory on stopping. It is easy to lose whoa or collection on a horse that is competing at high rates of speed, so constantly work on this. Switch to a bit that has more length to the shank to give you more whoa. I have found that sore hocks cause a horse to quit rating barrels because it hurts to use their hind legs, especially in deep or heavy ground. Check with your vet about this possibility.

Resisting Bit Pressure

The next commonly asked questions concern horses that open their mouths to escape bit pressure.

QUESTION I wanted to say thanks for sharing your knowledge with those of us who can't attend your clinics. The question I need help with is concerning young horses. When you are teaching a young horse to collect and back off the bit, what is the best way to start getting them to flex without opening their mouth and lugging on the bit? When I stop him or try to get his nose collected at the lope, he noses out and gaps his mouth open. He has a decent stop on him other than doing this. How do I enhance his collection and get him to quit opening his mouth? Thanks for your time.

QUESTION I have a horse that I have been running without a tie down. Everything is good, but when I added a cavesson, she constantly tosses her head. Why is she doing this?

Thanks a million. I will eagerly await your response.

ANSWER Let's address the first question. When a horse opens his mouth, he is attempting to get away from bit pressure inside his mouth. Instead of giving to the bit and adjusting his body properly to stop, collect himself, or whatever you are asking, he opens his mouth to relieve the pressure. You need your horse to respond to pressure in a positive manner, and opening his mouth is not correct.

We can correct this by putting a cavesson on. A cavesson is generally made of leather and fits snuggly down low on his muzzle above the bit and corners of the mouth. It is not really tight, but definitely snug so he can't open his mouth. First put him round the pen, bitted up with the cavesson on, to show him he cannot open his mouth. He is not going to like this much, so give him some time to adjust. This will definitely make your bits more effective.

In the second case, the horse probably is confusing the cavesson with a tie down and looking for that tension normally associated with that nose pressure. If you have this problem, put a tie down on that has a built-in cavesson.

Leaning in Your Turns

It is very important you do not lean in your turns. I see this often and know the horse's problem is because of his rider. You must stay in the middle and keep yourself really balanced. If you are shifting and moving around, you get in this horse's way as he is trying to use his body. He has to compensate for what is going on up there in the saddle while you shift his center of gravity around. He will have to compensate in some action, during the turn. Get into position and then sit still in the saddle till your body passes the barrel. Don't hinder what your horse is trying to do by getting him off balance. Push yourself into your saddle, get your weight in the outside stirrup, and hold your position, keeping your ears, shoulders, hips, and heels lined up.

Maintain your position
in the turns.

Remember to overexaggerate the correction of your problems and make your horse understand what it is you want. Do this by rewarding or petting him and by releasing pressure when he does what you want. These horses are hard to ride precisely, that is why we have to work so hard at it. Of all those good pro runs that get made out there, few of them are ever perfect. That is how difficult it is to be precise.

When evaluating any problem, remember how the run felt, watch a video of yourself, and ask someone that knows you and your horse best what they saw. Give it a few hours and it will come to you exactly what went wrong. The beautiful thing about barrel racing is there is always another one to go to. Have confidence in yourself and your horse that you can fix the problem before the next race, and you will go into the next run with confidence that you have done your homework correctly.

Prepare to Run

There are two types of competition runs: runs at home that simulate a competition run and the actual runs we will be making in competitions.

Let's start with those we do at home. Many barrel racers don't make enough competition-type runs at home. If we can't do it here, chances are we won't be able to do it when it counts.

So, one day per week, when he is far enough along we need to put ourselves and our horse in this situation. The day I make a competition run, I warm up for three miles, just like I do at the competitions. Then dismount, clean your horse's hooves out, put on leg wraps, and tighten your cinches while your horse's respiratory rate returns to normal, between five and ten minutes.

Wrapping Legs with Polo Wraps

Use polo wraps and bell boots to protect your horse's legs. Start with a front leg. Begin up under the knee and place the edge of the wrap

The photos below show how to wrap the right front leg. Note the direction and the ankle angle. It is not necessary to go too low on the ankle.

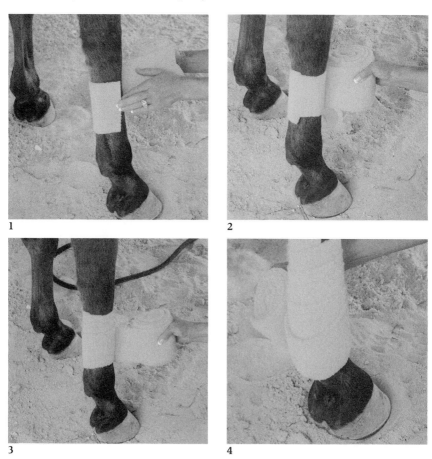

1

2

3

4

either on the inside or outside of the cannon bone. Wrap in a clock-wise direction on the right leg and a counterclockwise direction when wrapping the left leg. To remember which way, say, "Wrap to the left on the left, wrap to the right on the right." Look at the hair on your own arms and wrap the direction that it grows.

Wrap with enough tension so the wraps will not sag or get loose and slide down the leg: just enough to stay up and be comfortable. Wrap around the cannon bone one and a half times to anchor the polo wrap, then begin wrapping downward, applying even and fairly firm pressure. Most of the pressure should be applied when you come across the front of the shin instead of pulling forward against the tendons.

Overlap each wrap about one-third the width of the wrap. At the ankle, wrap the front edge of the bandage high, above the bottom of

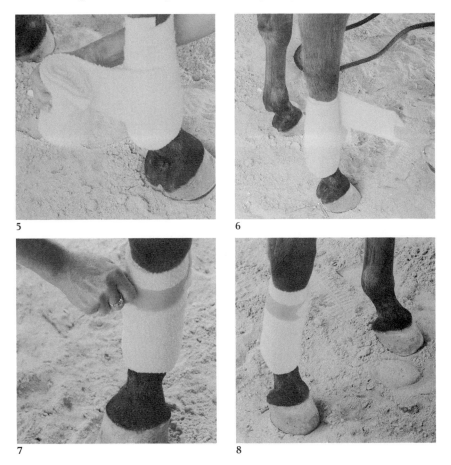

5   6

7   8

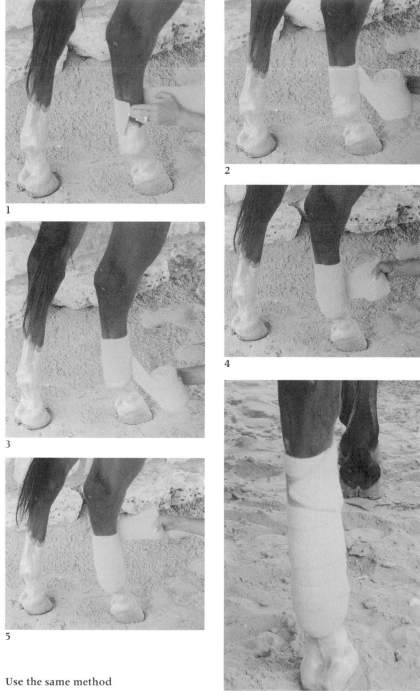

1

2

3

4

5

Use the same method
to wrap the hind legs.

6

the fetlock joint. Drop the bandage down and under the back of the fetlock joint and then back up in front. This will form a inverted "V" at the front of the ankle, giving room for the fetlock and pastern to flex. Continue wrapping back up the leg, keeping the wraps parallel to the ground and the tension even and moderately firm. Finish just below the knee or hock. Fasten the Velcro closure. For extra security, reinforce the closure with a strip of electrical tape. Don't apply the tape tight enough to indent the wrap. It is merely to prevent the Velcro from coming undone.

The hind legs are wrapped the same way, but because the cannon bone is longer, you need to start halfway down the cannon bone so you will end up just under the hock. Wrap all four legs for protection during competition.

Put on the bell boots, tighten your cinches, check headgear and reins, mount up, and get ready to make a run.

Approach the starting point, known as the hot zone. Stay relaxed. Keep one hand on the reins and relax your knees. Sit deeply in your saddle. This is how to approach a competition run every time. Horses are creatures of habit, so practice perfect and create good habits. Start lining up with your third barrel, lightly and smoothly adjust your hands twelve inches apart, lean forward, and start your competition run. If you have problems, go on with it and adjust along the way. Don't pull up if something goes wrong. Keep riding, correct your problem as you go, and focus ahead to where you want your horse to go. You are simulating a competition run, and there are going to be imperfections along the way that you are going to have to deal with.

After your run, bring your horse to a stop slowly by circling off to one corner; come back and face the pattern, get off, uncinch, and let your horse relax. Remove his polo wraps and hand walk him around the barrel pattern, checking out your tracks.

If the run was not good, don't punish your horse. Chances are it was pilot error. It normally is if our horse has been properly schooled on the basics. If you had applied everything correctly, you should have made a good smooth run. Look at your tracks and review your run. Analyze what you did correctly and what you didn't. Then use this information to correct your mistakes in this practice session by walking back through the pattern and analyzing what you and your horse could have done better. Until next week's competition run, focus on practicing perfect and knowing you fixed the problem as best you could. Make the next run with confidence.

Again, we have to apply this pressure to both ourselves and our champion horse at home. If we don't, when we get to a competition and ask a horse to do something we have not tried before, more than likely several problems will pop out. This is part of the seasoning process, and patience is the best friend you have. If you ride a young horse, he won't yet have the education or the hours of practice under his belt. You can't expect a four- or five-year-old horse to do a mature horse's job. He will make mistakes until he has experienced all the different conditions. You must be patient and give a young horse a chance to become an adult.

The Real Deal

Now let's talk about the real deal: competition. You arrive at the rodeo or the barrel race. If you stayed overnight, you took great care of your champion horse, and he is rested and ready to roll. You've arrived at the event with plenty of time to check in, evaluate the arena and the ground conditions, and get your game plan together.

It is time to put all that "practice perfect" stuff to good use. Do your normal thing, just like at home.

You have an established pattern and warm-up ritual you're comfortable with, and so is your horse. You do it the same way each and every time. This is old hat and you can do it in your sleep. While you effortlessly get ready, begin your mental preparation.

Groom your horse, then get him saddled and bridled. Begin with your warm-up. Ride three miles before the race to ensure you have plenty of extra speed today. One mile of trot, a mile of lope (a half-mile on each lead), and another mile of trot. Make sure your horse is listening to your voice and cues. Check that he is flexing, stopping, backing, and moving off your legs. This is not the time to tune him up or nag at him. It is too late for that. This is just a "preflight check," so to speak.

About fifteen minutes before my turn, I get off my horse, clean his feet out, wrap his legs, put on his bell boots, and cinch him up to competition tightness. I hand-walk my horse around, staying calm and relaxed, going over my game plan in my mind. About three to five riders before my turn, I get on my horse and stand till my turn, or if I have figured out my horse does better moving around, I will do that.

The Champion Run

When it is my turn, I take a nice, big, deep breath and let my hard work pay off. When I come down the alley, I'm relaxed. I keep my legs off my horse, letting them hang there, loose and relaxed. My hands are relaxed, with just the fingertips of one hand on the reins. The other hand is hanging at my side, nice and relaxed. I sit deeply in my saddle, and I don't pull on my horse. This is the way you want a horse to come into this run. I'm not saying they all will, but this is what you strive for. I am thinking nothing at this point; my mind is clear so it can talk to my body.

I line up with my third barrel just like in practice, reach up with my other hand, lean forward, and go. My chin is up, and I have my mind and eyes on the path that I want my horse to take to get around the barrel. I think and look way out front toward my first barrel. I do not allow the horse, that may be dancing under me, to take away my concentration.

About ten feet out, I sit deep in my saddle and say "easy." When my horse's nose is even with that barrel, I release my outside rein and push myself deep into my saddle. I take a hold of his bit with my inside rein while I arc his body with my inside leg. My weight is in the outside stirrup. I hold my position steady while looking out in front of my horse's nose, watching the path I want to take. When my body passes by the barrel, I ask him to run with my voice and outside leg. When his hip passes by the back side of the barrel, I reach up with my outside hand and move him over for the second barrel. I then use both of my legs by kicking or squeezing and go straight to the pocket of the second barrel.

I focus on the line I want to take and drive my horse directly to it. Ten feet out, I sit deeply and say "easy." I collect his stride, and when his nose is even with the barrel, release my outside rein, push on the saddle horn, tip his head and neck with the bit, and shape his body with my inside leg. The weight is in my outside stirrup, and I hold my position steady. When my body passes the second barrel headed to the third, I ask him to run by using my aids. When his hip passes by the barrel, I reach up to my outside rein, straighten his head and neck, and squeeze him over with my outside leg. I am in perfect line with the third barrel pocket, and I drive straight to it. My chin is up; I'm looking straight between my horse's ears, ahead at the line I want to run.

About ten feet out, I sit deep in my saddle and say "easy." When my horse's nose is even with the third barrel, I release my outside rein, pushing myself deep into my saddle. I take a hold of his bit with my inside rein while I arc his body with my inside leg. The weight is in the outside stirrup, and I hold my position steady while looking at the path I want my horse to take. When my body is facing the finish line, I ask him to really accelerate. When his hip passes by the back side of the barrel, I put my outside hand on the rein, straighten his head and neck, and squeeze him with both legs until I get to the end of the arena or alley.

I remain looking straight ahead. I drive for that alley opening or for the back fence of the arena. I ride all the way across that line and hear the announcer call out my time, and it is the fastest time of the race.

This is what champion ways are all about: putting all the pieces neatly and accurately in their place. You have just put that final piece in place. The picture is complete, and you are a champion.

Epilogue

There is no happiness except in the realization
that we have accomplished something.

—HENRY FORD

NOW THAT you have finished this book, I hope you can recognize, understand, and implement each of these time-tested pieces of the puzzle for your own success.

Through a lifetime of learning, I know the importance each piece plays in the overall champion picture.

With patience, dedication, and a desire to be the best, you will find yourself growing and improving until you have reached your goals successfully. Of course, I hope you will set more exciting, new goals to reach.

Within each set of goals that are planned, worked at, and obtained you will find the secrets to being a champion in all that you do.

I hope that I have helped you shorten your path to success, to avoid obstacles, and inspired you to realize that the sky is the limit.

Best of luck,

Marlene

Glossary

BIOMECHANICS The study of the mechanics of a living body, especially of the forces exerted by muscles and gravity on the skeletal structure during a function such as locomotion.

BROKE Gentled to ride with a saddle.

CANTER OR LOPE Both words are the same, a three-beat gait that is faster than a trot, and slower than a gallop or run.

CONFORMATION Body proportions in relation to one another. The shape or contour of the body or any particular body structure.

CROSSFIRE The hind leg is not in the same lead as the front leg.

FORM TO FUNCTION Visible physical shape or configuration and the manner or relationship it depends upon to make an activity, task, or purpose natural to its design.

4D BARREL RACE Four divisions of barrel racing. 1st division winner is the fastest time of the whole event; 2nd division winner is one-half second slower then the fastest time; 3rd division winner is one second slower than the fastest time; and the 4th division winner is one and one-half second slower then the fastest time of the whole event.

4-H For children nine to eighteen years old, to learn leadership skills, how to judge, show, demonstrate, care for, keep records on horses.

GAG MOTION The amount of distance the mouth piece of the bit moves up and down the shank

GALLOP A three-beat gait that is faster than a canter or lope and slower than a run.

GYMKHANA Standard events on horseback: key hole race, pole bending, etc.

HORSEMAN A man or a woman who rides and trains horses.

IMPULSION Driving forward with force.

LOCOMOTION Movement or the ability to move from one place to another.

LONGEVITY Duration of service; length of usefulness.

NAVICULAR DISEASE Ailment of the front foot, due to inflammation around the small navicular bone inside the foot, just behind the junction of the coronet and coffin bones.

PLAYDAY OR SHODEO Games on horseback; like egg race, spear the potato, carry the mail.

POCKET The amount of distance between your horse's body and the barrel.

PONIED When you ride one horse and lead another beside you.

RUN The fastest gait a horse can go. My favorite speed!!!!

SHANK Side piece on a bit that the mouth piece attaches to.

Resources

Associations

American Quarter Horse Association AQHA: www.aqha.com
American Paint Horse Association APHA: www.apha.com
American West 4D: aw4d.com
Better Barrel Races: betterbarrelraces.com
Barrel Futurities of America: www.barrelfuturitiesofamerica.com
Little Britches Association: www.littlebritchesrodeo.com
National Intercollegiate Rodeo Association: www.collegerodeo.com
National High School Rodeo Association: www.nhsra.org
International Pro Rodeo Association: www.iprarodeo.com
Women's Professional Rodeo Association: www.wpra.com
National Barrel Horse Association: www.nbha.com
Appaloosa Horse Association: www.appaloosa.com

Informative Web Sites

www.MarleneMcRae.com
www.ebarrelracing.com
www.horsecity.com

www.rodeoattitude.com
www.barrelhorsenews.com
www.WPRA.com
www.worldchampiondesigns.com
www.WoodysFeed.com
www.rodeovideo.com
www.nrsworld.com

Acknowledgments

I WISH TO thank my husband Douglas McRae, because without him I would never have written a book or shared my interest with others. He unselfishly pushes me to be the best, and I appreciate him for that. I love you and thank you!

I owe a very special thank you to Sugar Kuhns, who came to my rescue when their was no end in sight. She has been a long-time friend, and when I called upon her to help me write this book, she did just that. I could never have done it without her help.

As for others that have given there help and insight, I thank you. I am talking about Stacee Meis, Dan Deweese, Kenneth Springer, Kendell Oakleaf, and my parents, Carl and Elma Schiffer. I must thank all the students that have attended my clinics or taken private lessons from me. I have learned so much from you and your horses by watching you ride. It has taught me to put words to actions, and I will always be willing to help you understand your horses.

I thank Charles Henderson for introducing me to his agent Bob Markel. Bob has held my hand and explained how the world of writing and publishing works.

And finally to The Lyons Press for being patient and allowing me the time to put my thoughts on paper. Thank you for making this type of information available to all the people that love their horses.

Index